Argentina
1. Mount Fitz Roy Trail

Chile
2. Torres del Paine Circuit

Panama
3. TransPanama Trail

Peru
4. Inca Trail

*This map is for illustrative purposes only.
Trails are not shown to scale and are not intended for navigational purposes.

Austria
1. Via Alpina

Belgium
2. The GR5

England
3. Coast to Coast Walk
4. England Coastal Path
5. North Downs Way
6. Offa's Dyke Path
7. Hadrian's Wall Path
8. Pennine Way

France
9. The GR20
10. Pyrenees High Route
11. The Haute Route
12. The GR5
13. Via Alpina

Germany
14. Via Alpina

Holland (The Netherlands)
15. The GR5

Iceland
16. Laugavegurinn Trail

Italy
17. Alta Via 1
18. Sentiero Italia
19. Via Alpina

Liechtenstein
20. Via Alpina

Luxembourg
21. The GR5

Monaco
22. Via Alpina

Norway
23. Gudbrandsdalen Path

Scotland
24. Saint Andrews Way
25. West Highland Way

Slovenia
26. Via Alpina

Spain
27. Camino de Santiago de Compostela

Sweden
28. Kungsleden

Switzerland
29. The Haute Route
30. The GR5
31. Via Alpina

Turkey
32. Saint Paul Trail
33. Lycian Way

Wales
34. Wales Coast Path

*This map is for illustrative purposes only. Trails are not shown to scale and are not intended for navigational purposes.

GREAT HIKING
TRAILS *of the* WORLD

GREAT HIKING
TRAILS *of the* WORLD

80 TRAILS • 75,000 MILES • 38 COUNTRIES • 6 CONTINENTS

KAREN BERGER   *Foreword by* BILL McKIBBEN

American Hiking Society

RIZZOLI
NEW YORK

New York Paris London Milan

CONTENTS

PREFACE

By Gregory Miller, PhD • President, American Hiking Society, 2005–2016

Trails offer people from all walks of life boundless opportunities to enjoy nature, renew themselves, and establish a lifetime of fitness. We frame our own perspectives of the natural world through how we were introduced to nature as a child. Everyone who knows and understands nature, loves their trails, and explores the natural world on their own terms has developed this deep connection through place. My parents allowed me to catch frogs and snakes, climb trees, and join them on long, exploratory hikes in the hills and mountains of Southern California.

For me, the forests, mountains, and lakes of the San Bernardino Mountains inaugurated my lifelong journey through nature and underscored the timeless importance of connecting people and places through hiking. In 1936, my grandfather and grandmother, Claire and Elizabeth Dutton—a painter and housewife living in Alhambra, California, with their seven kids (one of them my mother, Bettie)—had a dream to improve the quality of their family life and spend more time in the mountains above the booming Los Angeles Basin. My mom and her siblings would come up the mountain to enjoy the fresh air, swim in the lakes, and hike in the forests. There were no electronics to pass the time, just fun outdoor recreation and horseplay. The legacy of these family adventures contributed mightily to my own love for the outdoors and my deep connection to place, specifically this place.

After countless family sojourns in these mountains—which were formally protected and preserved for all future generations to enjoy by the creation of the San Bernardino National Forest in 1893—I later went on to hike many miles along the Pacific Crest Trail and backpack the wilderness areas of Mount San Jacinto

(10,834 feet) and San Gorgonio (11,503 feet), including summiting these peaks, which are two of the most topographically prominent peaks in the United States. It was this rich hiking experience that motivated me to later hike the John Muir Trail in California, and many sections of the Inca Trail in South America. Seeing and feeling the extraordinary biological, cultural, and scenic richness offered by these trail corridors helped contribute to my love of nature and my professional path as an ecologist and conservation executive.

Great Hiking Trails of the World covers some of the most legendary trails on earth. Each trail has a dedicated constituency that embodies the local societal values, works tirelessly to build and maintain the paths, and speaks out for the conservation and stewardship of these priceless gems. Millions of people are attracted to these special places to discover the scenic, cultural, and historic heritage of each country, helping both locals and international visitors to establish a lifelong connection to the natural world and a love of the outdoors.

Most of us will find that hiking even small sections of these iconic trails to be a piece of paradise. Some years ago, I took my daughter's Girl Scout troop for a weekend campout and hike on a small section of the Appalachian Trail—a first for all the girls. I described the history of the trail, its length and importance, and the fact that Congress had designated it a national scenic trail. The importance of this trail was not lost on the girls, and they felt like they were hiking on hallowed ground. As hikers, we know that trails are life-enriching places and that the myriad benefits of the human-nature contact are universal. So put on your hiking boots and let Karen Berger help you chart your next outdoor adventure.

Appalachian Trail,
Tennessee, United States

FOLLOWING SPREAD
Mount Fitz Roy Trail,
Argentina

FOREWORD

By Bill McKibben

We live on a planet. Important as this fact is in an age of global warming, it's the most easily forgotten of truisms. That's because we're used to the cozy places we inhabit—day to day, we can't see the curve of the world, can't feel its length and breadth. Unless, of course, we get out in it, which is precisely what these trails are designed for.

I've had the good fortune to walk a few miles—or many miles—on some of them. From Tasmania and New Zealand to Iceland and Canada (and much closer to home, in lush New England), I've wandered on paths like these, through desert and rain forest, up high escarpment and down deep into ancient crater. Some of them are exotic, at least to us—to see pilgrims prostrating themselves around the perimeter of Mount Kailash is to see into another world. And some are homey—I'll never forget the first time I followed the footpaths of England, climbing over stiles into pastures and walking past vegetable gardens.

But all of them are reminders of the extent and beauty of this planet we inhabit. A trail is a fine invention, a way to get you out of your house but also out of your head. You wander out along it, and soon the ceaseless mental chatter in the back of your brain might actually cease; soon the experience of vastness around you might remind you of your actual size; soon fatigue and hunger might remind you that your body is more than a container for your brain; soon the glory of the sun's rays refracted through late afternoon clouds might recall for you actual exaltation.

I'm convinced these sensations are more important now than ever, because they're rarer now than ever. Mostly we inhabit a digital world—more of our life is spent face to face with a screen than with another person, or with a landscape. We evolved for that contact but now we spend our time immersed in a very different, and lesser, reality. And so to have the invitation of a trail leading us forth into a different dimension is no small gift.

And of course that gift came from thousands upon thousands of people who built and maintained these paths. Without them, most people would not venture far into the out-of-doors. Simply striking out across the forest or field with no path to guide you is an acquired taste, and not easily acquired at that. The blaze on the trail is a way of saying: "Many have come here before you. This is the way. You are on track, and you can relax and take in the glory that surrounds."

The problem with a book like this is simply the recognition that there are many places one won't get to in a single, short life. That's bitter, but it's also sweet, because it's another way of saying this is a big planet we were born onto. Big and full of meaning, just waiting to be discovered.

Pennine Way, England

INTRODUCTION

By Karen Berger

By physiology, by definition, by evolution, by history, humans are a mobile species. The child who can't sit still, the office worker with back problems and creaky knees, the young adult with wanderlust, the armchair traveler with dreams: they are all acting on a desire to move, or suffering the consequences of staying still.

Humanity has always been a species in motion— migrating, hunting, exploring, trading, crusading, fighting, conquering, evangelizing, bounty hunting. But travel for pleasure is a relatively recent phenomenon in human evolution. It wasn't until well after civilizations settled and wealth accrued that those with means traveled for comfort and relaxation. Wealthy Romans built vacation homes in Pompeii, and by the late 1500s, the wealthy young men of Europe began gilding their education with what would later become known as the "grand tour"— a circuit of the capitals of Europe.

It has only been recently that travel—for pleasure, for recreation, for rest, or for adventure—has become mainstream, available to the middle classes of developed nations. With the right combination of gear, money, and planning, we can now go virtually anywhere we can imagine. We can sleep in hotels at the bottom of the sea, or in tents atop frozen mountain tundra; we can pay someone to guide us to the summit of Mount Everest, or to the interior of the Amazon.

Indeed, sometimes it seems that the entire segment of the world's population that can afford to be in motion is in motion, that we are all collecting and consuming travel experiences, making bucket lists, and boasting about our visa stamps. We book tours—to Mongolia, to the Yukon, to everywhere in between—that so thoroughly protect us from our destinations that we can return home a week or two later having uttered not one word in a foreign language. In the lexicon of the tourist industry, adventure comes in two flavors, soft and hard; the oxymoronic soft variety includes the expectation of clean sheets, gourmet meals, and maybe even a spa treatment or two.

And then there are those who walk. By the act of putting one foot in front of the other, those who walk enter into a world of discovery, whether it be the internal world of a pilgrimage, the external world of a grand wilderness that stretches toward the infinite, or the temporal world of history, where to walk means to step into the path of those who came before.

Walking takes us back to the very definition of what it is to be human. Yes, we have big brains and opposable thumbs; we are thinkers and builders. But as a species, we are walkers: we have trekked from our ancestral home in East Africa clear across Asia, over the land bridge to Alaska, and down the entire length of the Americas. Moving at a pace not much faster than two miles an hour, we have settled virtually every nook and cranny of the globe. The first humanoids left Africa and walked into Europe and Asia between 1.3 and 1.8 million years ago; *Homo sapiens* are believed to have migrated from Africa between 50,000 and 100,000 years ago. But it is only in the last 200 years that we have moved at a speed faster than our own two feet—or, if we were among the rich, the speed of an animal that could carry us. We are wired to see the world at two miles an hour.

Travelers frequently keep lists of where they've been. "We did Belgium," they might say, even if all it means is that they stopped to shop in Brussels en route from Amsterdam to Paris. If you want to join the Century Club, which recognizes those who have visited 100 countries, a quick pit stop is all you need. It is quite a different experience to "do" a country, even a country as small as Belgium, on foot.

The GR5, France

FOLLOWING SPREAD
John Muir Trail, California, United States

You could follow the GR5 through Belgium. It's an international *Grande Randonnée* (great hiking route) that starts in the Netherlands near Rotterdam and meanders eastward through Flanders, Wallonie, and Luxembourg, then swerves south through Lorraine and Alsace, briefly enters Switzerland, then rollercoasters through the French Alps to the Mediterranean Sea. The Belgian leg of the trip takes about two weeks, leading through Flanders fields and the forests of the Ardennes, where World War II pillboxes still stand hidden in the woods. Each town has monuments naming the dead, and old men will stop a random tourist to reminisce about their experiences with American troops in the war. You don't have to ask which war. You might detour to a monastery to buy the famous overproof beer, visit with a family in a farmhouse, taste a few varieties of the world-famous chocolate, or learn the idiosyncrasies of communicating in a bilingual-plus-a-few country.

You could, of course, learn all this from the comfort of a tour bus. But it is quite another experience to walk alone through a forest in the Ardennes, stopping to squeeze inside a pillbox bunker. It's surprising how small they are: barely room to stand up, with small slits to look through. You can imagine waiting for the munitions to explode, you can try to imagine how you might feel, what you might do. Unlike the soldiers of a century ago, you, of course, have the option of leaving. So you walk on—perhaps you consider the men who died here—and pass through fields where the first poppies of spring are waving in the breeze, fields where cornstalks are growing, as light-catching and crooked as anything Van Gogh could dream up. These are the kinds of things you see when you hike.

We often think of hiking as merely the physical act of moving through a landscape on foot. It is that, of course, but it is also much more. The trails described in this book are windows into landscapes—forests, mountains, jungles—but they are also windows into cultures and histories and mythologies. On the Japanese Shikoku Pilgrimage, the clothing and traditions are the same as they were 500 years ago. In the English Lake District, golden daffodils still cover fields near the home of William Wordsworth. On Alaska's Chilkoot Trail, the discarded possessions of people who ventured this way lie abandoned on the trail, just as they were left more than

100 years ago, a testament to dreams that were bent into a new shape by a new reality. On the Inca Trail, we see structures that reveal the spiritual worldview of a people for whom sky, earth, and the underworld were intimately connected in every part of daily life. At the leisurely speed of two miles an hour, we have time to take it all in, to ponder, to make connections between landscapes, structures, history, and people—especially people.

It seems ironic that travelers claim to value contact with local people when the realities of modern travel make authentic connections so difficult. The typical tourist's day is a series of encounters with people paid to have encounters with tourists: cab drivers, waiters, professional guides, and so on. And hotels are lousy places to meet locals. On an independent walk, encounters are different. Meals are served family style in alpine refuges. Communal living arrangements may not be luxe, but trekkers bond while trading travel yarns around a table in

a hut. In small towns, the traveler on foot may find himself the object of interest and the recipient of hospitality.

Walking is not the fastest way to cross a land, but it is certainly the fastest route into the heart of a place. Slow travel is deep travel, a fertile ground for random thoughts. As we walk through a Spanish field of sunflowers, all exactly the same height except for one in a thousand that rises a foot higher, we might ponder those outrageous individuals who, with mathematical predictability, dare to stand out from the crowd. In Iceland, we might consider a landscape of such outrageous proportions that we begin to understand why the vast majority of natives believe that elves assist travelers through this weirdly sculpted and weather-tossed terrain. As a way of travel, walking is, in a sense, a kind of Rosetta Stone—an essential clue to understanding a new field of knowledge.

Some of the trails in this book were chosen because of their spectacular surroundings. Others bring the hiker in contact with something more than scenic vistas and pretty alpine lakes; they connect the walker with history, culture, myths, and, perhaps most importantly, people. Some of the routes are historic travel routes, originally built for the simple purpose of getting from here to there: the trekking paths of Nepal, for example, have connected villages for centuries. Others, like the Appalachian Trail, are recreational paths, designed and maintained with hikers in mind, allowing access to historic sites, towns, villages, and farms where trekkers can connect not only with a landscape, but also with its history and culture. Some, like the Camino de Santiago de Compostela, are historic routes of pilgrimage, now used for some combination of soul searching, vacation travel, and personal challenge. And some, like the John Muir Trail, are purely avenues into spectacular landscapes that can be reached by no other way than walking.

Many of the walks in this book are longer treks of multiple days, weeks, or even months. Most of them offer plenty of opportunities for day and weekend hikers. Completing the nearly 2,200-mile Appalachian Trail, for example, is an enormous feat. But the vast majority of those who use the AT are day hikers: the trail crosses hundreds of roads, many of which have parking areas. Locals use the trail for quick getaways, while tourists to the region can hop on the trail for a quick half day and experience a new perspective about the soul of the land.

Otter Trail, South Africa

OPPOSITE
Continental Divide Trail,
Colorado, United States

FOLLOWING SPREAD
Baekdu-Daegan Trail,
South Korea

Choosing the trails to be included in this book was both a challenge and a delight, but it was also a bit of a gauntlet: there are thousands—tens of thousands—of great trails, long and short, and each trail has its advocates. The American National Trails System, for example, encompasses nearly 18,000 miles of national scenic trails, plus thousands of miles of recreation trails and historic trails. France, which is approximately the size of Texas, boasts 20,000 miles of long distance paths alone. The Alps of not only France, but also Switzerland, Italy, Germany, and Austria are laced with a network of trails that connect high-altitude refuges where visitors can sleep, if not in luxury, then at least in more comfort than a tent. New Zealand's eight Great Walks take in a variety of terrain that ranges from one of the wettest spots on earth to the sere and active volcanic landscapes of the central North Island to an almost Mediterranean climate at the north end of the South Island. England's National Trails are found throughout the entire country, and take in the ecological, cultural, and historic diversity of this island nation.

In the task of selecting trails, I relied heavily on my own experience of walking some 18,000 miles on trails all over the world. But no one person's experience is definitive, and there are far too many great trails for one person to have hiked them all. So I reached out to my fellow walkers in the Appalachian Long Distance Hikers Association, a group that has clocked literally millions of trail miles all over the world. Certain trails make it onto the list simply because they have achieved the status of iconic through some combination of their scenery, history, experience, and reputation. These are trails everyone who knows anything about walking would put on their list, and to leave them off would be contrary, or ignorant. Some of the trails are less well known, but offer unique insights into their landscapes, cultures, and histories. I collected information, and then I got on a few airplanes and I walked some more.

And that, in the end, is what this book is about: walking, then walking some more. The world, it turns out, is still a walkable place, if not everywhere, then certainly in many countries favored by travelers. And there is no better way to feel the essence of a place than from the ground up, through the feet, as you walk across the land.

CHAPTER 1

The WAY of the PILGRIM

We begin with pilgrimage. • Migrations and trade came first, of course—people traveling from here to there for a reason. Emigrants on the Oregon Trail, Roman legions marching to the edges of the empire, traders on the Silk Road: their routes exist today in our imaginations, on our maps, and sometimes, still, on the land itself. They were routes of expediency and necessity, but above all, they were routes designed to be traveled on foot—from town to town, from home to church, from this place where we used to live to that place where living will be better in the future. Our forebears walked to settle, to explore, to conquer, to escape. • Sometimes, they walked for God. • Pilgrimage may be the oldest form of recognized, ritualized walking; the use of specific paths for a spiritual, not utilitarian, purpose. Many of these paths have come down to us, some as historic relics, some as living paths that are still in use today.

Pilgrimage seems to be universal among religions: making a *Hajj* (a pilgrimage to the sacred Ka'ba in Mecca) is one of the five pillars of Islam and dates from the very founding of the religion. The Hindu faith has thousands of shrines where believers venerate one or more of their pantheon of gods; some of its pilgrimages take months to complete. Jews make pilgrimages to Jerusalem, as do Christians and Muslims. In Buddhism, the pilgrimage is part of the sacred quest for self knowledge and enlightenment; different branches of Buddhism have different prescriptions for how that enlightenment is to be attained. And in the Christian tradition, pilgrimages to sites made holy by the presence of the relic of a saint or the reports of miracles have been a prominent tradition almost since the death of Jesus. Indeed, it is estimated that there are some 6,000 known historic pilgrimage routes in Western Europe alone.

Like pyramids, with a lowercase "p," the tradition of pilgrimage seems to be one of those ideas that sprang to life, unrelated, in different places, but often in similar time frames. Many of these journeys gained credence in the Middle Ages.

The specifics of how a pilgrimage is to be conducted vary. Historically, pilgrimages were undertaken on foot. Sometimes the reason for walking was nothing more than a practical necessity: walking was the only means of transportation available. If the destination was two towns away, the walk was short; if it was two countries away, it was long. The point was simply to get to the sacred site. In other cases, the value of the pilgrimage was thought to increase with the level of physical deprivation and challenge. Walking was more arduous than riding a horse; prostrating oneself by creeping or crawling was more difficult than walking. Today, people still walk. Some prostrate themselves. Some ride horses or bicycles—or take taxis, cars, trains, and buses.

Walking was, therefore, a means to an end, not the reason for the pilgrimage. But pilgrims soon learned that the act of walking and the act of removing oneself from the rhythms of society are both paths to spiritual growth. The Japanese pilgrimage to Shikoku is formally structured around the spiritual growth that occurs through the discipline and arduousness of walking for enlightenment. In Europe, mountain monasteries or retreats encouraged contemplation and solitude, with courtyards and mazes specifically designed for walking. Pilgrimage became a combination of a path and a goal: the path is the road to enlightenment. The act of walking creates a readiness to open oneself to spiritual transformation. Attaining the destination adds another layer of grace.

Now, at the beginning of the third millennium, humanity has rediscovered pilgrimage. Faith-centered journeys are a fast-growing sector of the active travel market, with packaged pilgrim vacations that promise an authentic experience, spiritual growth, and adventure. In some years, more than 200,000 people receive the pilgrim's *compostela* certifying that they have completed at least 62 miles of Spain's Camino de Santiago de Compostela. And that is just one trail.

The increasing popularity of packaged pilgrimages notwithstanding, the point of a traditional pilgrimage had nothing to do with recreation. A pilgrimage in the Middle Ages was not a vacation. Indeed, life threatening and full of deprivation, it was almost entirely the opposite. Almost always, a pilgrimage involved challenge, sacrifice, and purpose.

Today's historic pilgrimages follow traditional travel routes. Unlike modern hiking trails, these routes were not designed for pleasure; indeed, they weren't designed at all. Rather, pilgrimage trails either followed established roads, or were pressed into the landscape by footsteps laid one upon the other. There was no concern for whether the switchbacks were too steep or whether the trail passed over the most scenic mountains. Nor was

Camino de Santiago de Compostela, Spain

GREAT HIKING TRAILS OF THE WORLD

there necessarily an official starting point: with no cars or planes or motors to shorten the distance, a pilgrimage started wherever the pilgrim started walking. As pilgrims joined together, tracks formed into paths that then formed into roads, much like rivulets feed into streams that feed into tributaries that feed into rivers. The routes of pilgrims converged into trunk lines. The most prominent of these have survived into today's world, some of them maintaining a living presence as modern-day pilgrims try to re-create the experience.

The centuries-old tradition of pilgrimage is an interesting fit with modern recreational culture. On the surface, pilgrims and hikers do much the same thing: they put one foot in front of the other and they walk. But hiking is a vacation, and pilgrimage is a quest. Modern pilgrims are sometimes hikers, and modern hikers are sometimes pilgrims. Where they share a path they also may come to share a purpose. Spiritual or personal

transformation can come whether a person is search of it or not. As walkers find meaning in the rhythms of the natural world, in the repetition of routine, in the beauty of the landscape, they may also find evidence, if one chooses to see it that way, of an almighty creator.

Pilgrimage may be a ritualized, social experience or it may be an iconoclastic, personal one. Often, there are certain ways certain things must be done. In Nepal, one walks on the left side of the sacred mani walls so that when one returns, walking in the other direction and again on the left, the circle is complete. On Spain's Camino, one carries a scallop shell—the symbol of Saint James, which identified the medieval pilgrim and served as a practical implement for eating and drinking. On Japan's Shikoku Pilgrimage, pilgrims wear a distinctive ritual outfit that harks back to their medieval forebears.

One of the biggest differences between the medieval pilgrim and today's pilgrim-hiker is the many choices

Cows along Camino de Santiago de Compostela, Spain

to be made almost on a daily basis. In medieval times, you couldn't just hop in a taxi and skip the next boring stretch on a wet rainy day. For many walkers, pilgrimage today is intensely personal and orthodoxy is optional. But that means living with the choices we make. Must one walk the whole way? Are shortcuts allowed? What about a night in a nice hotel rather than a snore-infested hiker hostel? Is anyone counting? Does anyone care? If a westerner raised in a Christian tradition joins a pilgrimage to a Buddhist holy site, what sort of transformation is expected? Are we merely on vacation, doing as we please when it pleases us? Or are we on a mission? Are there rules? To whom do we answer?

These questions sound absurd at a desk, in a city. Who cares, and why bother? But on a trail, there isn't much to do but watch the scenery, walk the miles, and think—about the landscape, about the challenge, about why we are doing what we are doing. Conversations about how we structure, value, and adhere to our various pilgrimages can last for many days.

The pilgrimages that follow are surprising, both in how they differ and in how they are so very much the same. The specific rituals might vary. Catholic prayers accompany the swinging incense at the great Cathedral of Santiago de Compostela; Buddhist chants are sung with the offerings of candles and incense on Shikoku. But pilgrims experiencing these rituals will have far more in common than their differences. These pilgrimages have survived for hundreds of years. That they have been growing in popularity over the last 30 or so years says something about their universality—and also about how the act of walking speaks to the deepest part of us.

Kumano Kodō, Japan

Camino de Santiago de Compostela

Spain

If you were an adventure-minded person in the Middle Ages, you would have had only a few ways to sate your wanderlust. With the necessary contacts, you might become a soldier. You could try your luck as a trader or, perhaps, an explorer. Or you could embark on a pilgrimage, in which you would commit to a journey of perhaps weeks or months to some faraway place of miracles.

Medieval Europe had thousands of such destinations, places where sins were forgiven, afflictions were cured, and visions were seen. And thousands of travel routes went to them. Most held only local renown; a few

View of Pyrenees
French countryside

OPPOSITE
Village of Castrojeriz

attracted believers from all over the continent. Three of Catholic Europe's most important pilgrimage sites were Rome, Canterbury, and the town of Santiago de Compostela in Galicia in northwestern Spain, where the remains of Saint James are said to be buried.

A pilgrimage had a specific purpose: it was a trade of sorts, a holy contract between the walker and his god. Life in the Middle Ages was short and hard and hellfires burned bright at the end of it. Pilgrims could make a deal: their fortitude, devotion, and suffering in exchange for God's indulgence. Neither saved by grace nor by works, the pilgrim was saved by walking.

The Camino de Santiago de Compostela—the Way of Saint James—is not a single path. More accurately, it is a network of trails, a funnel of routes that coalesce into a main trunk that leads to the Cathedral of Santiago de Compostela, where a daily mass announces and celebrates the pilgrims who flow in, sometimes at the rate of hundreds a day. The major route follows an old Roman road to Finisterre, the westernmost point in Spain, where hagiography tells us that the body of Saint James, covered in scallop shells, washed up on shore. The Milky Way is said to point the way. According to a common medieval legend, the Milky Way was formed from the dust raised by the marching feet of pilgrims; the word *compostela* means "field of stars." And conversely, the popular Spanish name for the astronomical Milky Way is *El Camino de Santiago*.

It is one of the most traveled paths in history—and one of the most popular long-distance hiking paths in the world today. Continuously traveled as a pilgrimage route since the ninth century, the Camino has waxed and waned in popularity—fewer pilgrims in times of

plague or war, more in times of plenty. Usage declined to near extinction in the waning years of the 20th century. By 1978, only 13 people claimed the *compostelas*, or certificates, that are given to walkers who complete a journey of at least 62 miles. Riding a bicycle for 124 miles also earns the honor. But after 1980, with the global rise in interest in hiking, usage began to increase. In 1987, the Camino was declared the first European Cultural Route by the Council of Europe; in 1993, it was inscribed on the list of UNESCO World Heritage Sites. In 2006, German television celebrity Hape Kerkeling came out with the best-selling book *I'm Off Then: Losing and Finding Myself on the Camino de Santiago*. Interest in the Camino soared; by 2014, the number of pilgrims who collected their *compostelas* topped 215,000. And in holy years—in Santiago, that means a year when Saint James's name day falls on a Sunday—even more people come; the record is 270,000 pilgrims in 2010.

Perhaps the first and most important thing to understand about this hike is that while it has all of the elements of a long-distance backpacking trip—long climbs, heavy packs, hiker hostels, sore muscles, soul-sustaining scenery, vagaries of weather and terrain, blisters, unpredictable weather—it is deeply rooted in the spiritual traditions of pilgrimage, with rituals that go back more than a thousand years.

The differences are evident in the very definition of what it means to hike the Camino. Unlike a hiking trail, which begins at a fixed trailhead, a pilgrimage on the Camino begins wherever you happen to start it. Pilgrims of the Middle Ages couldn't take a plane to a nearby modern city, or a bus to a town at the start of a trail. Their trail started where they happened to live and, as a corollary, the Camino therefore had no fixed length; indeed the Via Regia extended from as far away as Russia, across Western Europe, over the Pyrenees, to Santiago. Pilgrims who lived two towns away from Santiago could complete their pilgrimage in a few days. Those who lived in northern France or Germany might have to walk several hundred miles and be gone for many weeks or months. English pilgrims had a channel of roiling water to cross. As the various pilgrims from all over Europe drew closer to Santiago, their paths coalesced, wearing finally into the main artery that gave the pilgrimage a focus, as well as a sense of guidance and community.

Sheep along Camino de Santiago de Compostela

As in the distant past, today's Camino is actually several caminos, coming from different parts of France, Spain, and Portugal. Perhaps best known is the 426-mile French Way (Camino Francés), part of the old Via Regia. This was the historic route taken by French pilgrims, who often gathered together to start in the cities of Paris, Vézelay, Arles, and Le Puy. Today, it is common for pilgrims to begin journeys on either side of the Pyrenees Mountains, which form the border between France and Spain: either at Saint-Jean-Pied-de-Port or Somport on the French side, or Roncesvalles or Jaca on the Spanish side. Another Spanish route follows the Spanish coastline near the Bay of Biscay. From Portugal, the 370-mile Portuguese Way starts at the cathedral in Lisbon.

This is not a wilderness path. Those who cross the Pyrenees will have a challenging mountain experience, but most nights will be spent in villages, in hiker hostels known as *albergues*. As they cross forests, fields, and farmlands, pilgrims may spot scallop shells inscribed in ancient stone walls, indicating that an establishment has been welcoming weary travelers for hundreds of years.

There are rules to this pilgrimage, some traditional, some unstated. The issue of what is, and what is not, an authentic journey is a common one on long-distance trails. The first consideration is distance. By far the greatest number of pilgrims do only the minimum distance necessary to earn a *compostela*—62 miles being quite far enough for the tens of thousands of walkers who have never before undertaken a walk of this kind. But while the Catholic Church makes no distinction between those who walk 62 miles and those who walk 1,000, the pilgrims themselves certainly do: added miles equal added cachet in the pilgrim community. Beyond distance, there are other issues. Taking shortcuts, staying in expensive and comfortable hotels, or accepting help from a support vehicle are all regarded as somehow less authentic ways of completing the journey. On hiking paths such as the Appalachian Trail, such discussions are often ended with the admonition to "hike your own hike," a mantra that acts as a sort of group defense against those who would judge another hiker's choices.

That loosey-goosey feel-good motto has no traction in the tradition-bound world of the Catholic pilgrimage. Instead, on the Camino, these discussions are amplified by the number of people having them, the centuries it has taken to create the traditions, and the overarching mystery and authority of the Catholic Church, an ever-present hiking companion.

Those who hike longer distances look down on those who hike the minimum. Distance, though, is not the only way to be elite: true pilgrims, you might be told, walk rather than ride bicycles or horses. True pilgrims do the journey all at once, not in sections over the years. Like priests, true pilgrims do their devotions in poverty: they stay in *albergues*, not comfortable hotels; they eat cheap meals; and they carry all their gear, rather than use taxis and hiker services to drive their belongings from one town to the next. And true pilgrims are expected to clear their minds of worldly concerns—although that may be the most difficult requirement of all, as today's pilgrims fight the almost magnetic pull to post pictures on Facebook or check the stock market on their smartphones.

Modern reasons for the journey differ from hiker to hiker: to ponder, to meditate, to heal, to find respite, to commune with nature, to experience an alternate lifestyle with an unbroken history of more than a thousand years. But this is a hike in which the physical, the emotional, and the spiritual form an unbreakable triangle.

Regardless of where a pilgrim falls on the continuum of effort and devotion, all pilgrims share in being a part of a historic tradition. They are as recognizable in our place and time as the medieval pilgrims were in theirs. True, the details are different: the medieval pilgrim's woolen cape has been replaced by Gore-Tex jackets; the wooden staff has been replaced by Leki trekking poles; and the scallop shell—which was carried by medieval pilgrims as a utensil, a symbol, and to announce to bandits and brigands that they traveled under the protection of the king—has been replaced by a plastic Platypus water bladder. Today's pilgrims still carry a scallop shell of some sort, whether as a piece of jewelry, an emblem on a T-shirt, or an actual shell in their pocket. Medieval or modern, the uniform is recognizable. And the activity is the same.

The similarly ancient tradition of hospitality to and commerce with pilgrims continues, with hostels and restaurants promoting their offerings to pilgrims with the traditional scallop shell. Both hospitality and commerce are woven into the history of the Camino: although we often think of tourist commerce as a modern invention, medieval hostel keepers and souvenir sellers found

Cross monument at Finisterre (top left); Castile and León region near Belorado (top right); stone arched bridge in Galacia (bottom left); sculpture of pilgrims at Castile and León, Spain

FOLLOWING SPREAD
Spent sunflowers, Camino de Santiago de Compostela

lucrative possibilities in the pilgrim trade. Today, in some Spanish towns near Compostela, pilgrimage is the heart of the local economy.

But regardless of modern gear, souvenir T-shirts, and dime-store mementos, the core of the Camino remains sacred. The *compostela*, once a "get-out-of-jail-free card" for the afterlife of the faithful, is still awarded to those who claim religious motivation for their journey. To earn the *compostela*, most pilgrims carry a document called the *credencial*, which can be purchased at churches along the route and at some Spanish tourist offices. This pass, stamped in hostels and churches along the way to provide proof of the journey, entitles the pilgrim to inexpensive or free hostel stays. After presenting the *credencial* to church authorities in Santiago, the pilgrim can receive the *compostela*, which reads:

> *The CHAPTER of this holy apostolic and metropolitan Church of Compostela, guardian of the seal of the Altar of the blessed Apostle James, in order that it may provide authentic certificates of visitation to all the faithful and to pilgrims from all over the earth who come with devout affection or for the sake of a vow to the shrine of our Apostle Saint James, the patron and protector of Spain, hereby makes known to each and all who shall inspect this present document that [Name] has visited this most sacred temple for the sake of pious devotion. As a faithful witness of these things I confer upon him [or her] the present document, authenticated by the seal of the same Holy Church.*
>
> *Given at Compostela on the [day of the month] of [month] in the year of the Lord [year].*
>
> *Deputy Canon for Pilgrims*

After receiving the *compostela*, pilgrims end their journeys at the cathedral, where their names are called out during the daily mass that celebrates the pilgrimage. So many pilgrims have laid their hands on the pillar just inside the doorway of the church that a groove has been worn in the stone. It is a tradition that marks, ends, and celebrates the journey—and that connects the pilgrims of today to their forebears in an unbroken tradition that goes back more than a thousand years.

SHIKOKU PILGRIMAGE

 *Japan*

The distance between Compostela, Spain, and Shikoku, Japan, is roughly 6,000 miles, a quarter of the distance around the earth. One country is a European peninsula, the other a collection of more than 4,000 Pacific islands. The language is different, the religion is different, the climate and topography—all different.

But what they have in common is far more interesting than their rather prosaic differences. Each has a pilgrimage that dates to the Middle Ages, and the similarities of these two journeys are in many ways—some would say, in the important ways—uncanny.

A short history: The Buddhist monk Kūkai sought enlightenment by walking around Shikoku, the smallest of Japan's four major islands. After attaining enlightenment, he became the founder of esoteric Buddhism in Japan. In the ninth century, his disciples began following in his footsteps, starting the tradition of a formal pilgrimage to be undertaken by priests. In 1687, a guidebook was published that brought information about the pilgrimage to everyday people. As it was a time of relative peace, commoners took to the trail to seek their own enlightenment, to look for cures for afflictions for relatives, to honor the spirits of dead relatives, to pray and reflect, and—in some cases—to escape from the poverty of their everyday lives.

Interest in the pilgrimage continued to spread. Mid-20th-century technology, namely bus tours, made the pilgrimage accessible to older tourists seeking a contemplative experience. Then, in the 1990s, the increasing global interest in hiking and pilgrimage brought Shikoku to international attention. Today, approximately 150,000 pilgrims, known as *henro* and often addressed *o-henro-san* as a title of respect for their devotion, annually complete visits to all 88 temples.

As on the Camino, the medieval Shikoku pilgrimage was fraught with uncertainty and danger, and pilgrims were identified by what they wore and carried. Camino pilgrims wore heavy protective capes; Shikoku pilgrims wore white garments that both protected them from the elements and could also serve as a burial shroud should the journey prove fatal. On the Camino, the traditional wooden staff was used for protection and support. The Shikoku pilgrim carried a staff too, but here the concept of support is both more literal and more spiritual. The

Temple washing fountain,
Shikoku Pilgrimage

OPPOSITE
Yakuoji (Temple 23),
Shikoku Pilgrimage

staff, called *kongō-zue*, represents the presence of Kūkai and the support he gives as he walks with the pilgrim. Similarly, both pilgrimages included emblems as part of the pilgrim's uniform: on the Camino, the *coquille Saint Jacques*—the scallop shell that represents Saint James; on Shikoku, a bell-festooned stole that pilgrims don when entering a temple. The sound of gently tinkling bells is an accompaniment to the pilgrimage, and a reminder that its purpose is beyond that of a mere hike. Shikoku pilgrims may also carry prayer beads, incense sticks, and coins to be used as offerings in the temples.

There are several acceptable ways of completing the pilgrimage. Travel by bus is acceptable, as is travel by taxi, motorcycle, and bicycle; also acceptable is completing the pilgrimage over the course of several years by visiting a few temples at a time. By far the majority of the visitors travel by bus. But, as with the Camino, pilgrims quietly rank one another. Those who walk the entire 750-mile route to all 88 temples in one trip—approximately 5,000 people each year—are considered the purest pilgrims, except, perhaps, for those who additionally visit some of the 200 or so other island temples, called *bangai*, which are not among the enumerated 88. The number of people doing the trip on foot has increased sharply since the 1990s, mirroring the pattern on other long-distance walks worldwide. In the case of Japan, pilgrimage offers respite from a lifestyle that is increasingly urban, crowded, and stressful.

Spring, when the cherry blossoms are blooming and the temperatures are still mild, is one of the most popular times to don the pilgrim's outfit of lampshade-style hat, white jacket, staff, and bells and strike out on the two-month journey. The pilgrimage is traditionally done in a clockwise direction, and generally follows the perimeter of Shikoku, passing through all four of the island's prefectures. The route roughly circumambulates the island, sometimes next to the coastline, sometimes zigging and zagging into the mountains. In spring, the pink cherry blossoms contrast with bright green rice paddies that glow with the newborn colors of spring. In the fall, changing leaves frame roadside shrines. The pilgrim follows city streets, roads, trails, and paths to travel from one temple to the next. In between, most pilgrims stay in towns, sometimes in inns, sometimes in private homes. The people here are well aware of the

pilgrimage; there is a long tradition of hospitality and respect toward the *henro*.

Before embarking on the journey (and also after completing it) many pilgrims visit Mount Kōya, which was settled by Kūkai and remains the headquarters of Shingon Buddhism. From there, the traditional start of the journey is at the temple at Ryozenji. Pilgrims make an offering of candles, and, as the incense and candles burn, they chant to cleanse the body, mouth, and mind. Prayers are made for completion and for wishes to be granted. A ritual of washing, making offerings, and chanting prayers will be completed at each temple along the route, all according to a strict formula.

It is traditional to consider the journey in four sections; each segment represents a stage that will be recognized by anyone who has completed a long hike. First, there is the breaking-in stage, where the shocking initial pain of walking all day unnerves all but the hardiest or

OPPOSITE

Typical old Japanese lanterns, Shikoku Pilgrimage

Statue of Kōbō Daishi, the ancient monk who originated the Shikoku Pilgrimage route (above left); statue of Jizō at a temple along the route (above right)

most experienced walkers. Next, there is the learning stage, as walkers find that they can push through the discomfort and develop a new rhythm in this very different environment. The third stage is a feeling of security and competence accompanied by an appreciation for one's surroundings. And finally, the fourth stage grants the ability to flow and be utterly at home in what was only a few weeks ago a new and challenging environment.

These segments are neatly articulated by Shikoku's four prefectures. Temples 1 through 23, in Tokushima, represent the starting point—the awakening of faith and the decision to embark on a spiritual journey. There is nothing easy about this. A particularly steep and challenging section of the route, between the 11th and 12th temples, is called "Pilgrim's Downfall" in honor of the hardship.

Temples 24 through 39, in Kōchi, represent austerity and discipline. The paths of this coastal route delve in and out of coves, climb up and down the surrounding hills overlooking the ocean, and probe into the very cave, named Mkurdo, where Kūkai himself meditated to find enlightenment.

Enlightenment is the theme of temples 40 through 65, in Ehime. By now, pilgrims will be hardened to the rigors of the journey. Routine has been established and thoughts can move from the everyday concerns of comfort, pain, and survival to more spiritual concerns. A sense of competence and comfort sets in. The terrain here is mountainous, with dramatic rock formations that bring to mind even earlier times, when the mountains themselves were considered deities.

And finally, temples 66 through 88 in Kagawa represent nirvana and the grand finale, as pilgrims reach temple 88, Kūkai's birthplace at Zentsūji, where wishes are said to be fulfilled.

It is a fitting end. And it only stands to reason that the pilgrimage should not be walked in reverse order.

Gokurakuji (Temple 2),
Shikoku Pilgrimage

40

GUDBRANDSDALEN PATH

Norway

At the beginning of the second millennium, a man with the sort of super-human energy one associates with Shakespearean protagonists, operatic kings, and insane politicians wielded a blood-stained axe through Northern Europe. He married women hither and yon, performed miracles, converted a pagan people to Christianity, and finally died in battle under the waning light of a full eclipse of the sun at the age of 35. And from there, his reputation grew for the next 400 years.

His name was Olav Haraldsson. Also known as King Olav, Saint Olav, Olav the Fat, and *Olav Rex Perpetuus Norvegiae*—Olav, Eternal King of Norway. Olav was an unlikely saint, known more for brutality than piousness. At the age of 14, he joined a group of Viking marauders who traveled to England, where he murdered Alphege, the Archbishop of Canterbury, by striking him with an axe. Olav became a Christian five years later, after spending time at the court in Rouen in Normandy. The dead Alphege became a saint—giving the pair a unique relationship in which one saint was martyred by the other.

But Olav was known for miracles as well as murders: he is said to have killed a sea serpent and thrown it onto a mountain, where its remains were ingrained in the cliffs. Another miracle was recorded as he died on the battlefield, trying to reclaim the throne he had lost two years earlier: a blind man regained his sight after rubbing his eyes with hands stained with Olav's blood.

And the miracles continued even after his death. Olav's followers hid his body when he died, and after a year, he was disinterred. Reports spread far and wide that the king looked as if he were only sleeping: his hair and nails had grown, his skin was fresh, and even his smell was pleasant and sweet. The miracle was immediately recognized, and Olav was locally canonized in Nidaros (now called Trondheim) in 1031. A church, later rebuilt

and expanded as Nidaros Cathedral, was built over his burial site. In 1164, his canonization was officially confirmed by the pope.

Stories about the miracles spread as far afield as England, where a church in York was named for him, and Constantinople, where another church was dedicated. In Iceland, his miracles were writ into the Icelandic sagas. As pilgrims started to arrive at Nidaros seeking miracles of their own, they too spread stories of the lame who could now walk and the blind who could now see.

Nidaros was now, like Lourdes, a place of healing, joining Canterbury, Santiago de Compostela, Rome, and Jerusalem as one of the most important pilgrimage destinations of the medieval world. For the next 450 years, pilgrims would come here from all over Northern Europe.

The Protestant Reformation changed all that. The Protestants had no use for relics, indulgences, or any other ritualistic trappings of Catholicism. The Danish Protestant authorities removed Olav's remains from the cathedral and quietly reinterred them, perhaps somewhere on the grounds. In 1603, pilgrimage became illegal. But by now, Olav was firmly entrenched in Norway's cultural iconography, entwined with Norwegian independence and national pride. The sainted Olav remained "Norway's King Forever," his battle-axe sunk into the nation's coat of arms.

Today, six *pilgrimsleden* (pilgrim's paths)—all called Saint Olav Ways—lead to the Nidaros Cathedral. Together, they add up to about 1,240 miles of walking paths. The 399-mile Gudbrandsdalen Path is the longest. It begins in Oslo and heads northwest, primarily following well-marked footpaths, dirt tracks, and sometimes country roads. This route, which takes from 30 to 35 days, is the most popular of the *pilgrimsleden*, although popular here is a relative term. Quite unlike

A cross marking Saint Olav's Trail with a view of Gudbrandsdalen

FOLLOWING SPREAD
View of Gudbrandsdalen Valley north of Lillehammer

the Camino, it is still unusual to find fellow travelers who are walking the entire trail.

The route itself is ancient, dating before even the time of Olav. In use as a trade route as early as the Iron Age, it is speckled with the remains of Viking settlements. It is also known as the Old King's Road, because virtually every Norwegian king has traveled this way; indeed Norway's Princess Martha Louise made a secret 31-mile pilgrimage to Trondheim with her future husband in 2002.

The route was largely abandoned after 1877 when a railway came to the region and offered a new, faster, and much more convenient way to get to Trondheim. In 1997, concomitant with the rise of worldwide interest in long walking paths and pilgrimage routes, the Norwegian government decided to resuscitate the path as a way to showcase Norway's cultural and natural heritage. The trail was waymarked, and six pilgrim's information centers were set up in Oslo, Trondheim, and at four more points along the way. In addition to maps and travel advice, the centers offer a useful *Overnattingsguiden* (lodging guide) and a pilgrim's passport, which functions much the same as the passports on the Camino in Spain or the Shikoku in Japan: stamps can be collected from churches and lodgings along the route, and those who have completed at least 62 miles may request an "Olav Letter" in recognition of their journey.

The landscape along the trail is a combination of farmlands, forests, valleys, ridges, subarctic tundra, and fjords. Starting from Olso, walkers must choose one of two routes along the eastern or western shores of Lake Mjøsa. The eastern side passes through bucolic farmlands as well as the town of Hamar, with its ruins of a medieval cathedral. The western side has a trump card: the birthplace of Saint Olav at Bønsnes, and the Sister Churches at Granavollen. The routes rejoin each other a few days into the trek near Lillehammer, the site of the 1994 Winter Olympics.

The path then heads up Gudbrandsdalen Valley, over the Dovrefjell Mountains, and down the Oppdal and Gauldalen Valleys, alternating between expansive wildlands and cozy villages. Some hamlets are little more than a cluster of farms; others contain open-air museums showing different aspects of Norwegian life—both medieval and modern—and traditional cuisine (always of interest to a long-distance walker). Near Sel, the

Jørundgard Middelaldersenter is a mock 12th-century farm that was originally built as a film set and now offers housing as well as live performances and an outdoor museum. Farther north, in Budsjord, there is a re-creation of a 14th-century bishop's farm.

Tombstones, historic markers, and medieval buildings—some of which are mentioned in medieval accounts of the pilgrimage—are a constant reminder of the past, and a few buildings are said to have sheltered pilgrims dating back to the 14th century. Today, hikers can find lodging in bed-and-breakfasts, inns, traditional *gapahuker* (open shelters), or some 50 hostels.

In between the hamlets, the high-latitude landscape is sometimes reminiscent of Alaska, sometimes of Scotland, with an undulating path—often strenuous—over hills, through spongy tundra, across rock-strewn valleys, and over wild, wind-battered moorlands. The weather can turn quickly from uncomfortably hot temperatures to subfreezing sleet and bone-chilling winds. Interestingly, written accounts from the medieval period record people traveling on snowshoes and skis, staying in high mountain huts supplied with wood and built with the purpose of sheltering pilgrims in periods of bad weather. The winds, we are told, blew the snow down into a hard-packed surface over which it was possible to travel. Modern hikers are either softer or more sensible: the hiking season today runs from mid-May to mid-September.

At the end, there is Trondheim, the capital of the region known as Trøndelag, just 500 miles south of the Arctic Circle. Now a sophisticated hotbed for research and technology, Trondheim's historic roots lie in miracles and mystery, and its gothic cathedral is still the place where Norway's kings and queens are crowned. A rose window containing more than 10,000 individual pieces of glass beams down light. Olav is not here anymore; he is thought to be resting in an unknown grave, perhaps in the cathedral cemetery or the cathedral itself. No one knows exactly where he ended up. But he remains Norway's forever king. And the pilgrims still come.

OPPOSITE
Dovrefjell Waterfall,
Gudbrandsdalen Path

Dovrefjell Lake,
Gudbrandsdalen Path

HELAMBU-LANGTANG TREK

Nepal

The journey to Gosaikunda in the Himalaya just outside of Kathmandu is a pilgrimage wrapped in a trek. For the western trekker, the attraction is the high Himalayan scenery of the Langtang Valley and Laurebina La (*la* means pass). But for devout Hindus and Buddhists, the trek is something else entirely, a richly communal and spiritual experience that takes place every year in rainy August, when tourists are few and far between. To walk to Gosaikunda Lake in May, and then to repeat the trek three months later in August, is to have two experiences so different that it is almost impossible to believe they took place on the same trail.

According to Hindu scriptures and epics, Gosaikunda Lake is the abode of the gods. Not the ancient gods of another time and place, but the living gods of today. Shiva and Gaui reside here, in these mountains. The lake was created by Shiva: after he swallowed poison to save the world, he needed fresh water to soothe the pain, so he dug the lake with his trident. His head is the black rock in the middle of the lake.

Every year, at the August full moon, tens of thousands of pilgrims from Nepal and India come to Gosaikunda. Hindus come to bathe away, or maybe freeze away, their sins, and on the date of Janai Purnima, they change the sacred thread they wear around their necks or hands. Local Tamang Buddhists, some of them shamans, come here to perform rituals accompanied by dancing and banging drums. This sharing of sacred space is typical of Nepal, where Buddhist and Hindu holy places often intertwine. Buddhist prayer flags fly over Hindu temples, Hindu gods inhabit Buddhist shrines, celebrants recognize and sometimes borrow each other's deities, and tourists lean in to watch and sometimes participate.

The August full moon takes place in the heart of the monsoon, a time when tourists tend to avoid the trails. And indeed, if the aim is to photograph the Himalaya and rhododendron blooms, this is not the season to head into the high mountains. On the other hand, while few western trekkers take the opportunity to undertake an authentic Nepali pilgrimage during the monsoon, those who do will experience something quite different from the touring commerce that has imposed itself on the local cultures in Nepal's trekking regions in the last 30 years.

In some villages along popular Nepali trekking routes, almost all businesses now cater to tourists. Livelihoods depend on the whims of tourists and whether this particular trek in this particular country is on this year's list of trending travel hot spots. But

Gosaikunda Lake, Helambu-Langtang Trek

OPPOSITE

Approaching Laurebina La, which divides the Helambu Circuit from the Langtang Trek

during the Gosaikunda pilgrimage, the colors of North Face and Marmot jackets give way to the equally bright but differently patterned hues of traditional Indian fabrics and palettes, along with the turquoise, lapis lazuli, and corals of the traditional Buddhist women's jewelry. The sky may be subdued with cloudy mist, but the pilgrimage is a bright and colorful affair—if sometimes soggy. And it never goes out of fashion.

Regardless of season, a trekker in Nepal is rarely far away from the gods. It would be impossible to fail to notice the mani walls, chortens, stupas, prayer flags, and water wheels that line the trekking paths. Everywhere in the Nepal Himalaya, the motion of nature moves the thoughts and hopes of humans to the gods. Prayer flags—with colors representing the elements—yellow for earth, green for water, red for fire, white for air, blue for space—are strung at high passes, at the entrances to homes, on bridges across rivers, and from stupas, sanctifying the area and honoring the gods. The wind takes the prayers from the flags to the heavens. In rivers, streams of water flow over prayer wheels placed to catch the energy of the river; the turning motion sets the prayers inscribed inside the prayer wheels free to find their fate. On trekking paths, the hands of passersby spin wheels found tucked into the stone walls that line the trails; each wheel contains thousands of prayers written on paper. And the mani walls themselves are made from stones inscribed with prayers. The hiker is reminded to always walk on the left side of these walls, clockwise around them. That way, a full circle will be completed when they return the other way. Circles are important; they mean completion and wholeness. And although the non-Buddhist trekker may not collect karmic merit in the same way the local Tamang people do, the observance is a mark of respect that is appreciated.

Most trekkers visit in the dry seasons—either September through December or March through May. There are several ways to approach the Helambu-Langtang region depending on how much time you have. From a logistical perspective the easiest choice is to start at Sundarijal, about an hour's bus ride from Kathmandu. From there, the route leads into the Helambu region and up to 15,121-foot Laurebina La, from which you descend to Gosaikunda Lake. While Laurebina La is at a much lower elevation than hikers encounter on either the

Annapurna or Everest treks, it is high enough to cause altitude sickness for trekkers who haven't spent enough time acclimating. Volunteer doctors from the Himalayan Rescue Association man stations near Laurebina La, tending to trekkers who overestimated their ability to adjust to the altitude. During the pilgrimage season, they tend to pilgrims, who are just as likely to make the same mistake. From Gosaikunda Lake, trekkers can drop into the Langtang Valley. Following it upstream leads to a region of high peaks and enormous views, with only a ridge of high mountains separating Nepal and Tibet. The return offers a choice between taking different routes or backtracking via the same one.

It is also possible to start from Dhunche, which offers a gentler introduction to the Langtang region. However, getting to Dhunche requires a seven- or eight-hour bus ride—and bus rides in Nepal are not for the faint of heart. After experiencing bus trips Nepali style, many trekkers prefer to walk, or, at least, to minimize bus time when possible.

Taking the Langtang and Helambu regions together, a trekker could easily spend 17 or 18 days on a grand loop, although shorter treks are possible, especially if you come in or out via bus to Dhunche. The highlights of this trek are its variety—from farming villages and rhododendron forests up to the rock and ice of the alpine zone—and the chance to see the local Tamang Buddhist culture, which is closely related to that of the Tibetan Buddhists not far to the north. In addition, this trek is much less crowded than the better known Annapurna and Everest treks, even though it boasts competitive scenery and much more convenient transportation. It is an easy trek to do independently, and well-spaced teahouses make it possible to trek without carrying camping gear.

Hindu pilgrims, sometimes skimpily clad in flip-flops and cotton clothing, do come to Gosaikunda at other times of the year. Seeing them make their way along the sometimes snow-covered trails puts a different slant on the whole "what you need to buy to trek in the mountains" discussion. This is a journey that combines the spectacle of high mountains and the culture of a traditional people. It is a place where the spiritual world and the mountain world share the same space. And the essential connection with the landscape is common to pilgrims and trekkers alike.

MORE NOTABLE PILGRIMAGES

Jesus Trail, Israel

Starting in Nazareth and ending in Capernaum at the Sea of Galilee, Israel's 40-mile Jesus Trail takes walkers through the towns and places where Jesus did his ministry. Highlights include the Church of the Annunciation in Nazareth; the Monastery of the Transfiguration, where a transfigured Jesus is said to have spoken with Moses; and Cana, where Jesus performed his first miracle by turning water into wine (and where tourists can buy small bottles of "miracle" wine or stay at the Cana Wedding Guesthouse). Also on the route are the Mount of Beatitudes; the church at Tabgha, which commemorates the New Testament account of Jesus feeding the multitudes; and Capernaum, Jesus's home base on the Sea of Galilee (*Kinneret* in Hebrew). Other historic and biblical sites along the way include: Zippori National Park (site of the Crusader Church, and thought by some biblical scholars to be the village where Mary lived as a child); the Druze shrine of Nabi Shu'ayb (said to be the site of the tomb of Jethro, father of Moses); the Arab village of Mashhad (one of two sites traditionally held to be the grave of the Old Testament prophet Jonah—the other is in Iraq); Kibbutz Lavi (with a monument to Holocaust victims); and cliff dwellings where the historian Josephus tells us Jewish rebels hid from Herod the Great. The Israel Ministry of Tourism has recently opened another trail, the Prophets Trail, which is more or less parallel to the Jesus Trail. It stays in more natural areas, but in so doing, avoids many of the towns and historic or biblical sites. Choose according to your interests. Or do both.

Mount Kailash, Tibet

Considered sacred to four religions—Bön, Buddhism, Hinduism, and Jainism—Tibet's 22,028-foot Mount Kailish has steps that lead to heaven, and a summit where the god Shiva sits in meditation. Climbing the mountain is forbidden; it is said that those who try will die. But a pilgrimage around the mountain, called the *kora*, goes back thousands of years. To erase their sins, Hindus and Buddhists walk the 32-mile path clockwise; Böns and Jains walk counterclockwise. The trek is challenging, through a barren high-desert landscape with breathtaking elevations above 15,000 feet and a high point of 18,600 feet at Dolma La. Altitude sickness is a pervasive problem. Services along the trail are rustic, with only occasional teahouses and places where pilgrims can purchase supplies. Guide services allow foreigners to experience the pilgrimage, which takes about three days.

Jesus Trail, Israel

OPPOSITE
Mount Kailash, Tibet

North Downs Way, England

The pilgrimage to Canterbury Cathedral was one of the most important pilgrimages in the medieval world, undertaken in commemoration of the murder of Thomas Becket in 1170. Immortalized in Chaucer's *Canterbury Tales*, the Pilgrim's Way followed an ancient track that may have been used as early as 500 BC. The North Downs Way is a modern re-creation of the original route (much of which is now under the pavement of major highways). One of the English National Walks, this 153-mile trek passes through towns and villages with good rail access, and is easily explored as a series of shorter hikes. The main interest lies in the region's history, which is capped with a visit to the cathedral.

Saint Andrews Way, Scotland

According to the Gospel of John, Saint Andrew was a disciple of John the Baptist, and later preached along the Black Sea as far as Kiev and Nogorod. In Scotland, he is revered for having appeared in the eighth century to a Pictish king, Angus MacFergus, just as the king was retreating from the time-honored tradition of doing battle with the English along the Borderlands. In the king's vision, Saint Andrew promised—and the next day, delivered—victory. His symbol, a white cross on a blue background, appears on the Scottish flag, and his relics were housed in a cathedral in what became the town of Saint Andrews on the east coast of Scotland. Pilgrims, including kings, princes, and the nobility, began arriving in the 10th century. After a period of decline due to wars, the pilgrimage ended in 1559, when John Knox, the Protestant reformer, urged the pillage and destruction of the Catholic cathedral. The last 100 years have seen a remarkable resurgence of interest in the idea of pilgrimage in Scotland, concurrent with the rising global interest in long-distance walking worldwide. The historic pilgrimage was officially revived in 2012 as a network of paths. Dubbed the "Little Camino," it follows traditions that would be recognizable to pilgrims to Santiago de Compostela, including a pilgrim's passport. The first official route, Saint Margaret's Way, named after the 11th-century Scottish queen and saint, starts at the cathedral in Edinburgh and runs 62 miles to the massive hulk of ruins of the Saint Andrews Cathedral.

OPPOSITE AND BELOW
North Downs Way, England

FOLLOWING SPREAD
Saint Andrews Way, Scotland

Kumano Kodō, Japan

UNESCO includes only two pilgrimage routes on its World Heritage List. One is Spain's Camino de Santiago de Compostela. The other is the Kumano Kodō, a network of trails and ancient pilgrims' routes that connects iconic sites of Japanese Buddhist history in the Kii Peninsula. The mountains of Kumano, covered by thick forests, threaded by rivers and streams, and containing deep gorges and waterfalls, were the cradle of Japanese mountain asceticism, where priests who had undergone severe deprivations and physical hardship were considered to have supernatural powers. The section of trail recognized by UNESCO is a 25-mile, two-day mountain walk from Takijiri-oji, considered to be the entrance to the sacred area of Kumano and the mystical Kumano Hongū Taisha. Pilgrims today follow in the footsteps of aristocrats and holy men who traveled these paths hundreds of years ago.

Saint Paul Trail, Turkey

The 310-mile Saint Paul Trail follows the route the Apostle Paul is said to have taken on his first missionary journey to Anatolia. The red and white blazes lead over Roman roads, footpaths, and forest tracks. Starting at sea level, the trail reaches elevations of about 7,200 feet and offers opportunities to climb, via side trails, to two 9,200-foot peaks. Not only is the trail blazed, it is also digitized for iPhones, with GPS navigation data and information about nearby attractions and services. The main trail runs from Perge, near Antalya, to Yalvaç, near Lake Eğirdir; both Antalya and Lake Eğirdir are major transportation hubs. The entire trip takes about a month and is best done in spring or fall. Accommodations will be a combination of pensions, homes, and camping.

OPPOSITE

Kumano Kodō, Japan

Saint Paul Trail, Turkey

CHAPTER 2

STEPPING
into the PAST

Backpacking magazines rarely have buildings on their covers. There is, of course, a reason for that: in our imagination, hiking is about mountains, forests, and other wild places. And, in the American imagination at least, wilderness and human settlement are mutually exclusive. • No matter that the Appalachian Trail was conceived as a series of communities in the wilderness. No matter that hikers on any long-distance trail frequently form transient communities, some complete with customs, language, and rules. No matter that long-distance hikers love the respite of a town stop, and enjoy sampling local cuisine and taking in the sights. Nor that the high-mountain refuges that dot the European alpine landscape originated centuries ago as a way to make the mountains safe for people passing through them. Deep down, we think of hiking as being apart from humanity. • And yet, it is sometimes the juxtaposition of these two

opposites—civilization and wildness—that creates the most striking experience, the most lasting impression. Perhaps this accounts for the fact that some of the world's most popular hiking trails offer as much in the way of cultural exploration and history as they do of traditional wilderness.

Over the millions of years that have passed since humans first stood upright and started walking across the continents, our species has left its marks all over the world. Many trails—perhaps even most—bear the tracks of those who walked here long before anyone thought hiking and backpacking were something people might do for fun.

As a result, in Europe, hikers walk past museums, battlefields, war memorials, and ancient castles. In England, we learn that the concept of a national park encompasses not only mountains and lakes, but also farms, towns, and ancient estates, their boundaries marked in centuries-old stone walls. In Asia, trekking routes might take us past roadside shrines and temples or through villages still connected only by footpaths.

Even in the United States, where the cultural understanding of wilderness excludes humans, some of the national scenic trails tell us as much about history and culture as they do about wilderness. The 4,600-mile North Country Trail takes hikers through small-town rural Americana; the New England Trail passes 40 communities in its 215-mile path; the Natchez Trace is a historic route, first used by Native Americans and later used by traders; and the Potomac Heritage Trail follows the route the first European Americans used to migrate over the Appalachians toward what would become Pittsburgh and beyond.

One of the best ways to fully experience a country is to choose a hike that alternates between natural areas bursting with scenic vistas and wildlife and towns replete with historic and cultural sites. The focus can be on the present as well as the past: culture, after all, is a living, changing thing. Shared communal accommodations such as alpine refuges, hostels, trail shelters, and *gîtes d'étape* give travelers the opportunity to meet other hikers, some of whom will be residents of the region. And the less traveled the trail, the more interested local people will be in making the acquaintance of a stranger who enters their village on foot.

Too, the person who walks through a historic landscape is able to experience the past on a deep and visceral level. It is only in the last two centuries that humans have been able to travel at anything faster than the speed of a hiker or, at best, a horse. Walking through a landscape that our forebears traveled on foot—whether as soldiers or traders or emigrants—teaches us about their experience in a way that no book or guided bus tour ever can. Our feet tread the same ground, we feel the same sun, the same wind, the same cold. The same kinds of insects will torment us, our disappointment at a dry water source will be as acute, and our muscles will know how it feels to be at the last reserves of energy. We read about the supplies our forebears had to transport, and we feel their pain: we too know the burden of an overloaded pack and the relief that comes with shedding some of its weight.

The trails in this chapter walk through a combination of ancient histories and extant traditional cultures.

In Israel, we walk through towns whose names are familiar to us from temple or church, and from hymns and holidays. Not only that, but we walk in the steps of armies, prophets, and Jesus himself—all of whom traversed this land on foot. Our experience is equally rich in the present tense: as we trek across the desert through the Judean Hills of the Old Testament to the Galilee of the New Testament, we encounter some of the dozens of ethnic groups that make their home in this complex and colorful culture.

In Peru, we might feel more mystery: the spiritual worldview that is etched everywhere in the structures of the Inca is less familiar to us than the biblical names we find on the Israel Trail. But as we walk through the mountain landscape and respond to the rhythms of nature, the reverence this culture had for the natural world cannot fail to resonate. The Inca were walkers: they built nearly 20,000 miles of trails to connect their empire. The path we today call the Inca Trail connects the Sacred Valley with the holy citadel of Machu Picchu, hidden high in the clouds where the Andes pour water into the tributaries of the Amazon Basin. It is one of the most popular trails in the world. But the experience here is far more than just a matter of hiking up a mountain pass, or even learning about an ancient culture. It is also about learning how the beliefs and traditions of the past still inform the lives of the Quechua people—the direct descendants of the Inca.

And now from sublimity to sacrilege: in the Italian Dolomites, we have the unusual task of trying to imagine a peaceful mountain setting as a battlefield. If we were walking on part of the Alta Via 1 in the winter of 1916, we would be dodging gunfire. Today, as we walk past the old fortifications and tunnels, we can also reflect on how an infrastructure once designed for warfare—the famed *via ferrata* climbing routes—has been repurposed as a popular type of mountain recreation.

Similar historic detritus greets us on the impossibly steep slopes of Chilkoot Pass in Alaska and British Columbia. Here we might feel a visceral kinship with the men who, desperate to cross the pass and find their way to the gold fields, labored under enormous loads of supplies that would have to last through a subarctic winter. Some of what they left behind more than a hundred years ago still lies on the paths we follow over the same pass today.

And in Nepal, we watch as culture, trekkers, and the modern world collide in one of the most spectacular mountain landscapes on the planet. On the Annapurna Circuit, trekkers once followed paths used only by villagers on foot, donkeys, and yaks; today, a new road has catapulted a traditional subsistence society into the 21st century. The trekker today thus shares the trail with new tour buses, which have brought more people, but also more facilities and amenities. The towns and villages along the route are adjusting to the change; some of them prospering from the commerce, others creating new trekking paths so hikers who want to escape the road can take side trails to traditional villages. It is a study in contrasts that raises questions about the role of visitors, and the role of technology, in a traditional society.

An old saying tells us that to understand another person you must walk a mile in his shoes. We cannot ever duplicate another human's experience. Among other things, we have better hiking shoes today, not to mention better trails, better equipment, and better clothing. If all goes awry, we can, on most trails, usually bail out to a town and crawl into a hotel room. But even with today's amenities and options, the act of walking on a trail with a visible history gives us a more intimate understanding, not only of schoolbook history—with its countries and kings and dates and wars—but of some part of the experiences of individual people who passed this way, on foot, in another time, for another reason.

Annapurna Circuit, Nepal

ISRAEL NATIONAL TRAIL

Israel

Everywhere you look, you will see names you know. The street signs, the names of churches, even the names of hotels and businesses—all remind you where you are. They tell you that *this* is where it happened: King Nebuchadnezzar and his Babylonian army conquered the city of Lachish. Sarah and Abraham pitched their tents in the Negev Desert. The prophet Elijah confronted the false priests in the forests of Mount Carmel. John baptized Jesus in the River Jordan. The angel Gabriel came to Nazareth to tell Mary she would bear the son of God. Jesus walked on water at the Sea of Galilee, and turned water into wine at the wedding in Cana. And it all happened *here*. On what is now the Israel National Trail.

How appropriate: the Jews roamed the desert; Jesus walked to Jerusalem; the Three Kings traveled from afar. And now hikers traverse the same place, in the same way, at the same speed. The names, the places, the sense of mystery and history combine to create a resonance that can be felt by almost anyone who grew up in a western culture. It is something that etches the trail on the hiker's heart, the historian's mind—and on the pilgrim's soul.

The Israel National Trail is a remarkable project: a 620-mile-long hiking trail that showcases thousands of years of human history in a backdrop so isolated and wild that it might seem we have walked back into biblical times. It seems impossible that a tiny country with a square mileage smaller than that of New Jersey could have a trail that takes between 45 and 60 days to walk. The explanation lies in cartography, politics, and geography: cartography, because Israel is a long, skinny country, 263 miles as the crow flies, from north to south; politics, because the trail has to twist and turn to avoid potentially volatile zones such as the Golan Heights and the Green Line (the demarcation line that acts as a temporary border between Israel and the West Bank); and

geography, because the trail turns and veers to showcase the country's variety of landscapes—the Negev Desert in the south, the Judean Hills in the center, the coastal plain (also in the center), and the Galilee in the north.

Founded in 1995 with the Appalachian Trail as its inspiration, the Israel National Trail (*Shvil Yisra'el* in Hebrew) was designed to provide Israelis and visitors with a path into the entire country's astonishing range of environments and landscapes. It also showcases its history: up-to-the-minute excavations shed new light on towns that were settled thousands of years ago, while legends, myths, biblical stories, and historic texts speak of Assyrians, Nabateans, Babylonians, Romans, ancient Christians and Jews, Turks, Crusaders, English, and the multicolored, multicultural panoply that makes up today's modern Israel.

The colors of the blazes that mark the trail—orange, blue, and white—give some indication of what lies ahead: orange for the desert, blue for the sea, and white for the snow. Notably absent is green, although that decision is debatable: while there are long days where the land stays firmly in the beige, buff, and brown side of the color wheel, Israel is a country that has a national obsession with irrigating the desert and planting trees. And there is plenty of green in the well-watered north.

Traveling from south to north, the trail begins in the beige and brown palette, framed by the deep blue of the Red Sea for contrast. From Eilat, at Israel's southern borders with Egypt and Jordan, the trail climbs 2,000 feet into the stark, sometimes savage sand mountains of the Negev Desert. The Negev is the realm of seminomadic Bedouins and their camels, now often put to use for tourist rides. Wildlife includes long-horned Nubian ibex, antelope, onagers (Asiatic wild asses), deer, foxes, hyraxes, and (rarely) wolves, along with the Israeli mole

Makhtesh Ramon, the world's largest erosion crater, Israel National Trail

FOLLOWING SPREAD
Ein Avdat, just off the Israel National Trail near the historic ruins of Avdat

viper and the deathstalker scorpion. More reliably seen than wildlife are spring wildflowers—one of the natural displays around which many hikers schedule their walking itineraries. Water shortages in some sections of the Negev make careful planning, and sometimes water caching, necessary. Continuing north, still in the desert, the trail crosses the multihued, heart-shaped Makhtesh Ramon, which, at 25 miles long, one to six miles wide, and 1,640 feet deep, is the world's largest erosion crater and Israel's largest national park. The trail also passes through the ruins of the city of Mamshit, where you can walk through alleys, temples, and the remains of stables, houses, and administrative buildings left behind by the Nabateans, spice traders who brought frankincense and myrrh from South Arabia to the Mediterranean Sea from about the third century BC until the second century AD. From Arad, hikers can take an easy side trip to visit Masada, where Jewish martyrs perished in a mass suicide atop the desert rock fortress in defiance of the Romans.

The trail then climbs into the heart of Israel: the more populated and much greener Judean Mountains near Jerusalem, with town names that echo back to biblical times. It passes the "Burma Road," which was used during the Israeli War of Independence to provide supplies to besieged settlers in Jerusalem. From here, a two-day side trip via the Jerusalem Trail leads to the capital. Once back on the Israel Trail, hikers head west to the Mediterranean coastal plain, then north along the sea, passing near modern Tel Aviv and historic Jaffa, and continuing on through ancient Caesarea, built by King Herod, of murderous biblical fame.

Turning inland again, the trail climbs through the Mount Carmel Forest and reaches the town of Isfiya, which is built on the remains of a fifth-century Jewish town and has Crusader ruins, but is today inhabited by Druze, who make their living from olive oil, grapes, and honey. It then cuts east, passing Nazareth and the Sea of Galilee. As the trail heads north, the climate becomes wetter and greener. At the western arm of the Jordan Rift (part of a gigantic rift system that extends to the Great Rift Valley of East Africa), it overlooks the Hula Valley, where some 750 million cranes and other birds migrate every year on journeys between Africa and Northern Europe and Asia. The trail ends in the city of Dan near the Lebanese border.

There is also a distinct trail culture here, an idea that was imported from the Appalachian Trail, but has thrived in the desert soil to grow into something unique to Israel. Trail angels, an idea also imported from the Appalachian Trail, have become an institution: called "Malachim," these are people in towns, villages, and kibbutzes near the trail who feel a connection with hikers, and who help in emergencies, assist with logistics such as caching water and supplies, and provide shelter and meals, sometimes at no cost.

The environmental variety and history would be quite enough to earn the Israel Trail a spot on "best trails" lists worldwide. But the trail is as much about the current culture of Israel as it is about the past, whether that current culture is a gay pride celebration in Tel Aviv, a traditional Orthodox Shabbat, or an Arab post-Ramadan feast. Israel's living culture is as fascinating and multidimensional to explore as anything found in history books or bibles: messy, colorful, noisy, vibrant. Hikers experience the all-encompassing silence of the desert, the busyness of a working kibbutz, and the bustle of multicultural cities where people of different nationalities and ethnicities go about their lives. This is a country that manages to pack thousands of years of history, scores of cultures, and a diversity of ecosystems into an impossibly small space. On the Israel Trail, every step leads to new perspectives and revelations about one of the world's most sacred spaces.

OPPOSITE
Historic Jerusalem (top left and top right); ruins of Caesaria, built by King Herod, in central Israel (bottom left); trail sign in the Judean Hills (bottom right)

Negev Desert in southern Israel

INCA TRAIL

Peru

You will want to arrive at the Sun Gate early in the morning. You will be standing high above Machu Picchu, looking down at the geometry of ruins and terraces, and the sun will rise as you descend to the holy citadel. You will have walked four days to get here. If you have had a good guide, you will have learned that Inca culture was intimately tied to natural cycles: sunrise and sunset, changes in seasons and planting cycles, movements of the stars and planets. You will know that the duality of the sun and the moon, and the trinity of sky, underground, and land, were sacred. You will understand the symbols: the condor, which represented the sky—the abode of the gods; the snake, which represented the underworld—the realm of the dead; and the puma, which represented the land of the living. You will see these ideas and symbols everywhere in the iconography and architecture of the buildings down below.

The path that is known as the Inca Trail connects the railroad along the Urubamba River with the sacred mountain city of Machu Picchu. It is something of a misnomer: like the Camino de Santiago de Compostela, the Inca Trail was actually not a distinct trail, but part of a much larger network. In this case, the network included nearly 20,000 miles of trails built by the Incas to connect the far-flung outposts of an empire that reached from what is now Quito, Ecuador, to Santiago, Chile, to Mendoza, Argentina. The heart of the empire was in Cuzco, but its soul was at the sacred site of Machu Picchu. The 26-mile Inca Trail is the most famous of these ancient pathways, and one of the most popular hiking trails in the world.

Starting at the bridge at Kilometer 82 (the 51-mile marker on the train tracks from Cuzco), the Classic Inca Trail climbs into the Andes, and on the way passes the Inca archaeological sites of Runcuracay, Sayacmarca,

Machu Picchu, Inca Trail

Phuyupatamarca, and Wiñay Wayna. Most trekking itineraries try to time their arrival at Machu Picchu in time for the sunrise.

"It took my breath away. What could this place be? Why had no one given us any idea of it?" wrote Hiram Bingham, the American explorer who brought word of the rediscovered Lost City of the Incas back home to the United States. "No part of the highlands of Peru is better defended by natural bulwarks—a stupendous canyon whose rock is granite and whose precipices are frequently a thousand feet sheer . . . Yet here in a remote part of the canyon . . . a highly civilized people, artistic, inventive, well organized, and capable of sustained endeavor . . . built themselves a sanctuary . . ."

Access to the trail is strictly regulated. All hikers must trek with authorized guides (an added expense, but one that gives trekkers the distinct benefit of having someone who can interpret the symbols and meanings of the ruins along the trail). Permits must be reserved several months in advance. Even with quotas, numbers are high enough to create something of a mass-tourism experience: 500 people a day, including guides and porters, are allowed to start at Kilometer 82 and the Short

OPPOSITE
Footbridge near ruins of
Wiñay Wayna, Inca Trail

Llamas looking down toward
Machu Picchu, Inca Trail

FOLLOWING SPREAD
Inca Trail near Dead
Woman's Pass

Inca Route, a one- to two-day alternative trek that begins at Kilometer 104 (mile 65).

Hikers looking for a more solitary experience might investigate other itineraries: the Salkantay and Inca Trail Trek is a more rigorous seven-day hike that begins near the town of Mollepata and treks around the base of snowcapped Salkantay Mountain for three days before joining up with the Classic Inca Trail.

The Classic Inca Trail is rated moderate, which means that, with guides doing the navigating and porters doing the hauling, hikers need not have extensive experience, and anyone who is fit can handle the daily mileage. But that doesn't make it easy: some of the climbs are flat-out challenging, especially in rain and mud (and there is always plenty of rain and mud). Altitude sickness is a common problem. The classic four-day route goes up to about 13,800 feet. Taking time to acclimate before embarking on the trail will pay huge dividends in terms of comfort and enjoyment.

Note that Cuzco itself is at an altitude of 11,150 feet and many visitors get sick flying in from sea level. Two or three days' acclimatization in Cuzco or the Sacred Valley can make a huge difference in comfort and health on the trail. There is plenty to see in and around Cuzco—the cathedral and city center; the Museum of Qurikancha; the Inca ruins of Sacsayhuaman, Q'enko, Pucapucara, and Tambomachay; and, in the Sacred Valley on the way to the Inca Trail, the market town of Pisac and the Inca fortress at Ollantaytambo.

The Inca Trail can be hiked year-round except for February, when it is closed for conservation work. January through March is the rainy season; June through August is the high season. That leaves April, May, and September through December as the best months for hiking.

As a UNESCO World Heritage Site and one of the "New Seven Wonders of the World," Machu Picchu is by far the most important of Peru's travel destinations. While the Classic Inca Trail will no doubt remain on bucket lists of travelers worldwide, it is worth remembering those other 20,000 miles of trails the Incas built, many of them with ruins that are only just being rediscovered today. Some of them are open for trekkers, offering a more independent and remote opportunity to explore the high Andes Mountains, the history of the Incas, and the connection between tradition, humans, and the land.

CHILKOOT TRAIL

United States and Canada

Chilkoot Trail near
Sheep Camp, Alaska

OPPOSITE
Remnant of hauling
sled near Deep Lake,
British Columbia

Hauling a 40-pound pack over an arctic-alpine pass on the border of Alaska and British Columbia? Backpackers have it easy compared to the so-called stampeders, hopeful gold miners who struggled over what was once called the "meanest 33 miles in history." Those who could afford it hired Indian packers to haul their gear over 3,500-foot Chilkoot Pass. Those who could not were forced to fend for themselves, climbing and descending the pass dozens of times, each time with 50 to 60 pounds on their backs, in order to pass muster with the Canadian authorities waiting at the top. That meant a 700-foot elevation gain on the approach from sea level—then a fast brutal climb of 2,800 vertical feet in about three-and-a-half miles. Images of Sisyphus come to mind.

The rationale was simple: in 1897, gold had been discovered 300 miles south of the Arctic Circle, near Dawson City in the Yukon Territory. By 1898, word had gotten out and miners were streaming into the Yukon— the US National Park Service estimates that some 30,000 men, women, and children climbed over the pass. If you were going to cross the border into Canada on foot, float 500 miles down the Yukon River, settle in the middle of subarctic nowhere, and try to wrest your fortune out of the frozen, mercurial Klondike Gold Fields, the authorities wanted to know you had what you needed to survive on the frontier. The list of required food supplies added up to more than a thousand pounds a person; together with clothing and supplies, the total per person averaged close to a ton. To add insult to injury, Canadian customs officers collected duties at the pass. To cross the pass today, all you need is a permit and a strong pair of legs. You get the permits from the Parks Canada Trail Centre in Skagway, Alaska. The quota is 50 trekkers a day. The legs are up to you.

The hike begins in Dyea, Alaska, a few minutes' drive from the port city of Skagway, and climbs alongside the Taiya River crossing bog boardwalks and suspension bridges, then rising through coastal rain forest up into subarctic forest. At the seven-and-a-half-mile mark, Canyon City greets hikers with a warming cabin and the remains of gold rush building foundations, rusted-out restaurant stoves, and an old boiler. Four miles farther is Sheep Camp, where thousands of miners waited their turn to start up the pass. The Scales, where provisions were weighed by packers, were known as "one of the most wretched spots on the trail." Many stampeders

became discouraged here, discarding their equipment, drowning their sorrows in one of the restaurants or bars, and turning back for the coast. Rusted artifacts lie everywhere, reminders of abandoned hopes. Those who continued still had to confront the "Golden Staircase" in the alpine zone—snow covered, windswept, frigid, and treeless. The final half mile is a climb of 1,000 feet, a 40 percent grade on scree, shale, and snow. Guide ropes and steps were cut into the snow, but there was a fee to use them. Some stampeders took a month or more to haul the required food and gear to the top. Like modern hikers starting a thru-hike with too much of the wrong stuff, they discarded what wasn't needed. Today, those bits and pieces of refuse are now considered artifacts, and the trail itself known as the world's longest outdoor museum.

From the pass, it's all downhill. But no matter how heartfelt your sigh of relief, it is likely to be a pale imitation of what the stampeders felt as they finally started the descent. An overnight stop at aptly named Happy Camp is followed by a long, slow hike to Lake Bennett in British Columbia.

The hiking season, quite sensibly, extends from late May through early September. Stampeders, however, weren't so sensible. In a frenzy to reach the fields where they hoped to make their fortunes, they tried their luck at crossing whenever they happened to arrive. And indeed, some found winter crossings to be easier. Bogs froze in the cold, and snow on the mountain hardened to form a walkable, packed surface over the enormous boulders that otherwise blocked the path like an obstacle course conceived by the devil. Some didn't make it, dying of hypothermia, falls, and avalanches. Today's hikers generally take three to five days to complete the hike, traveling south to north (the direction in which the prospectors traveled) and ending at Lake Bennett, where they can reward themselves with a hot meal at the historic Bennett Eating House followed by a scenic train ride back over White Pass. The stampeders? Their work wasn't close to being done: they still had to build themselves a boat and float another 500 miles down the Yukon River.

View west from
Chilkoot Pass, Alaska

ALTA VIA 1

Italy

It is a strange way to climb a mountain—from the inside. The tunnel ceiling is low. The ground is uneven, with high steps carved into the floor. Along the wall a metal cable is bolted into the rock, a welcome handrail for support. It's mostly dark, except for the tiny points of light from hiker headlamps. Sometimes, a window is cut into the outer wall, from which you can stop and look out over the valley or across to steep mountain walls. At various points along the way, you can peer into what would have been quarters for officers or enlisted men. If you stop to catch your breath, you might consider what it would have been like to live and fight here, in the guts of the mountain, throughout the frigid winter of 1915 to 1916.

An 86-mile hiking trail, Alta Via 1 is the best known of the numbered *alta via*, a network of high trails that cross the Dolomites. These are dramatically serrated mountains, smaller than the Alps, but with a striking verticality of enormous rock walls and fantastic pinnacles. But beyond the scenic mountain landscapes, the Dolomites also offer the unique opportunity to walk through a World War I trench warfare battlefield.

The battle to control the high passes of the Dolomites along the Austrian-Italian border in World War I was one of the most prolonged and brutal alpine battles in history. The Dolomites formed the border between the two countries, and for two years, Austrian and Italian soldiers were stuck in a grim standoff, battling not only each other but also the mountain winter, and fighting their way through an unforgiving vertical landscape that killed via falls, frostbite, hypothermia, icefall, and avalanches.

Monte Lagazuoi, elevation 9,000 feet, is the highest point on the Alta Via 1. As one of the key fortifications held by the Austrians, it was the site of some of the fiercest fighting in the alpine winter war. The Italians tried to take it from the inside, creating a network of tunnels that

San Antonio Path, Alta Via 1

could be used to ferry troops and supplies—or to blow up enemy positions.

Climbing to Lagazuoi, hikers pass the remains of encampments: parts of buildings, trenches, cooking equipment, century-old tin cans, bits of barbed wire, and the remains of rock buildings once used as redoubts. At the popular *rifugio* perched on the rocky summit, hikers can explore an outdoor museum via the trenches and tunnels from which Austrians fired down on the attacking Italians, sometimes dangling over empty space to toss a grenade down on the attackers. While you're there, you might see a reenactor dressed in the uniform of a World War I soldier, or watch as a group of schoolchildren led by a nun wearing a full habit and hiking boots starts down the trail. And sitting on the deck of the rifugio, enjoying hot soup, a glass of wine, and the unparalleled view of the passes below, you will understand why it was so important to hold this strategic commanding position.

Another legacy of the war are the *via ferratas* (literally, iron paths). These protected climbing routes offer an experience somewhere between hiking and rock climbing. The original via ferratas, usually consisting of ropes, ladders, and wooden stemples, or steps, were built to enable Italian alpine military units to move through the mountains. After the war, climbers began using these routes, which were gradually improved by the Italian Alpine Club. Today's via ferratas use steel cables, steps, ladders, and bars that are bolted and cemented into the rock, allowing access to routes that would otherwise be inaccessible to all but technically skilled rock climbers. Growing environmental concerns have slowed the growth of new via ferrata routes worldwide, and in the Dolomites, the Alpine Club now concentrates on protecting and restoring already existing routes rather than making new ones. But with its historical connections, more than 130 routes, and the highest concentration of via ferratas in the world, the region is a major destination for this kind of climbing.

The Alta Via trails do not require hikers to attempt a via ferrata; there is always a "normal" hiking option. But for those interested, the Alta Via 1 offers several opportunities, either as an alternate to the trail or as a nearby side trip, to experience this unique way of moving through the mountains. One of the most interesting is the Lagazuoi Tunnels. With steel cables that are used mostly as handrails for support and balance, this route can be considered a "via ferrata lite."

Via ferratas are rated by grade (although various guidebooks disagree on the specifics). Newcomers should start well below the level they think they might be comfortable with, especially if trekking independently. The Lagazuoi Tunnels are rated easy, but whether it is easier to tackle them downhill or uphill is arguable, depending on the state of a hiker's knees and lungs. Most guides recommend downhill because the steps are high enough that climbing them becomes a real chore. Even so, with uneven steps, a low ceiling, wet footing,

OPPOSITE
Braies Lake, starting point
of Alta Via 1

Forcella de Lech Path,
Alta Via 1

and darkness, less experienced hikers may find either direction tough going. A headlamp is necessary and a climbing helmet is strongly recommended. Guided groups use harnesses on some sections, but most independent trekkers are more likely to simply hold the cables for support (in which case a harness is not needed, but a trekking pole will be a big help). Along the way, hikers will see barracks used by both enlisted men and officers, as well as openings blasted into the rock that provided ventilation and allowed supplies and munitions to be brought up by cable. Another historically interesting alternative for the descent from Lagazuoi is the Kaiserjaeger Trail, an easy via ferrata that also passes relics of the fighting—but stays outside the mountain, in daylight. At the bottom, the Museum of the Tre Sassi Fort at Passo Valparola tells the story of vertical trench warfare in a brutal winter mountain climate.

Hiking the Alta Via 1 is not for the faint of heart (or lungs). Depending on mileage, a day's walk can include elevation gains of more than 3,000 feet. But there is a soft bed at the end: the vast majority of hikers on the Alta Via stay in rifugios, which offer a combination of private, semiprivate, and dormitory rooms with blankets, pillows, hot showers, and occasional Internet access. Hearty meals reflect the region's mixed Austro-Italian-Ladin heritage; pasta is ubiquitous, but so is *apfel strudel*. Bunks or rooms should be reserved in advance, especially during the summer high season. Most hikers do smaller sections of the trail; those who complete the entire route take anywhere from eight to 12 days.

Hiking any of the Dolomite Alta Vias means walking into an environment where there is a constant interplay between the power of nature and the fortitude of strong mountain culture. As you pass an old fort, or a pile of barbed wire, it is hard to conceive of a place less likely to be conscripted as a battlefield. And the mountains themselves were participants in the carnage, sometimes destroying the lives of Austrians and Italians, and sometimes being blown to bits. The stories and the remnants of war still litter these mountains; the tunnel systems and the scars blasted into the mountains will endure as long as the mountains themselves. Is it futile to hope that the idea of war will have a shorter lifespan than the stories and the scars?

San Antonio Path, Alta Via 1

FOLLOWING SPREAD
Pastoral companions along Alta Via 1 (top left); alpaca and Rifugio Scotoni on path to Lagazuoi (bottom left); high country near Lagazuoi (right)

ANNAPURNA CIRCUIT

Nepal

Trekking through wilderness has a specific meaning for most hikers: walking away from the human world into the natural one. Trekking in Nepal has always been quite the opposite: not an escape from culture, but an introduction to a different culture. The Annapurna Circuit is a 17- to 20-day trek that encircles the Annapurna Massif and takes hikers past some of the highest and most inaccessible mountains on earth. But it also introduces trekkers to a traditional culture that is rapidly changing, owing to increased contact with the trekkers, the relentless and irresistible spread of new technologies, and the introduction of a road that now links a previously isolated rural society to the outside world.

This represents a meteoric rate of change for a culture that was closed to foreign travelers until 1950. Even after foreigners were finally allowed to travel in Nepal, access to the rural regions was (and still is) strictly controlled. When the first mountaineers arrived in the 1950s, the only maps available to travelers were based on old surveys performed in secret by British cartographers, many of them from the previous century. (Much of the early part of Maurice Herzog's book on the first climb of Annapurna seems mostly concerned with the question of finding and identifying the mountain.) In the late 1960s, the counterculture arrived. The stoners congregated on Freak Street in Kathmandu; the nature children headed to the mountains. Tourists couldn't climb to the top of Everest or Annapurna. But they could trek.

What they found was a place where the trekking experience takes hikers to the root of walking: not walking for pleasure (although it is that) or for beauty (it is that, too), but walking as a means of transportation. Well into the 2000s trekkers on the Annapurna Circuit passed through villages where none of the residents had ever seen an automobile. The paths trekkers followed

were not recreational hiking trails; rather, they were functional routes that had been used for travel and trade for generations—since long before Nepal opened its borders and began allowing trekkers into its remote regions. Goods were brought in by yak, or by donkey, or on the backs of porters. Villagers visited other towns only by walking. When trekkers arrived, they too followed these traditional paths, eating and staying in teahouses whose history lay not in the commerce of foreign trekking, but in a culture of foot travel as transportation.

The traditional Annapurna Circuit starts at a roadhead near Pokhara and makes most of a circle around the Annapurna Massif, which comprises Annapurna—26,545 feet, the 10th-highest peak in the world—all the lesser Annapurna Peaks, and the famed Machapuchare (Fishtail Mountain). The route starts in semitropical vegetation, where terraced rice paddies shine a brilliant green on impossibly steep mountain slopes, and then climbs from village to village, up the Marsyangdi Valley, where Manaslu (the eighth-highest peak in the world) looms overhead. Continuing to climb, it enters the rain-shadowed plateau of Manang, a high-altitude desert of brown earth topped by white-cloaked mountains, then climbs even more, to Thorong La, which at 17,780 feet is the highest point on the trek. Dropping down, it reaches the sacred Hindu and Buddhist pilgrimage site of Muktinath, then enters the Kali Gandaki Valley, which, measured from the valley floor to the summit of the surrounding mountains (which include Annapurna to the west and Dhaulagiri, the world's seventh-highest mountain, to the east), is the deepest canyon on earth. Along the way, it passes through villages where prayer wheels spin, prayer flags flutter, prayer walls stand guard, and life goes on pretty much as it has for centuries. Until recently, trekkers on the Annapurna Circuit saw no cars,

Horses from a trekking group, Annapurna Circuit

no roads, no electricity, and no telephone lines, yet every night they could stay in a village, and every day they would encounter people moving along the trails at the same human pace as they.

The region offers spectacular opportunities for trekking: a basic infrastructure that can provide food and lodging, a path that is described in guidebooks so well that even moderately experienced hikers can follow it without a guide, and a range of environments from bamboo forest to desert tundra to high Himalayan passes that take hikers' breath away—sometimes, quite literally. Daily encounters with locals at teahouses—and sometimes even in homes—introduce trekkers not only to the mountains, but also to the mountain people.

In the 1990s trekking became so popular that environmentalists worried about the impact of too many

OPPOSITE

Annapurna South and Machapuchare from the trail

Farming settlement near Dana, Nepal

visitors on Nepal's culture and environment. Cultural concerns included the number of children who turned to begging, the change from subsistence rural economies to tourist-centric economies, and the erosion of traditions and values. Environmental concerns included the increased pressure on local resources (especially fuel wood), erosion and landslides, increased stress on the region's infamously poor sanitation facilities, and litter. And all this in a region where the mere idea of change was a radical concept.

It is ironic, then, that in the Annapurna region, the biggest recent agent of change is homegrown. In 2000, the Nepali government decided that all district headquarters in the country needed to be accessible by a road. In rural regions, this most often meant building on top of the traditional routes of travel. And in the Annapurna region, it meant the Annapurna Circuit itself became a road.

So change has come: hikers and villagers no longer share the road only with yaks, donkeys, and fellow walkers; they now have to dodge motorbikes, jeeps, trucks, and in some cases, tourist buses. The road has turned what was once one of the world's great remote treks into a tourism experience for anyone who can climb into a jeep. And the impact has sharply divided the communities along the Annapurna Circuit.

To be clear, the road that now almost encircles the Annapurna Circuit is not a major highway: it isn't paved, it has yet to cross Thorong La, and some of it is only accessible by motorbike and four-wheel drive. For those involved in farming and in any sort of trade, th e road is a godsend, for all the obvious reasons that roads exist all over the world. For trekkers, and for some of the villagers whose livelihoods have depended on trekkers for the last 50 years, the road has been more problematic. Short-term tourists are now flocking to more accessible areas (and, of course, heretofore unknown tourist amenities such as souvenir shops and Internet access are following in their wake). At the same time, long-distance trekkers who had once spent money in villages throughout the trail are now looking for alternate routes where they don't have to dodge jeeps and buses and walk in a haze of vehicular dust. For locals, this means a redistribution of tourist traffic that overcrowds some areas and takes business away from others.

But this is not a trek that can be written off quite so easily. First of all, the mountains are the same as they always were: some of the highest and most impressive on earth; awe-inspiring and too enormous to be captured in a photograph no matter how wide the lens. Second, the region offers alternative trails. One is the Annapurna Sanctuary Trek (otherwise known as the ABC, or Annapurna Base Camp Trek). This weeklong trek takes walkers into the high cirque formed by the Annapurna Massif, and the base camp, at nearly 14,000 feet. Annapurna's shimmering summit looms almost 13,000 feet above, poking into an impossibly blue sky.

Local trekking operators are not giving up. Work is progressing on marking and writing guides for a "new Annapurna Circuit" trek, an alternate route that loosely follows the general direction of the old Annapurna Circuit, but that deviates from the road whenever possible to follow paths to villages that remain accessible by foot traffic only.

Change is a fact of history. The Himalaya are growing at the geologically meteoric rate of about two-and-a-half inches a year. Tourism is growing, too; from 2001 to 2013, the number of tourists visiting Nepal rose from 463,000 to 798,000, many of them coming to do the major treks. The road around the Annapurna Circuit is inching toward Thorong La; when complete, it will be one of the highest roads in the world. While the traffic and vehicle tourists are no doubt intruding on what was once one of the most iconic cultural treks in the world, the area remains one of the planet's great mountain spectacles. The traditional culture is still vibrant and welcoming. And new routes that will recapture the old experience are in development.

That the Annapurna Circuit has changed is inarguable; whether the trekking experience can adapt is yet to be seen. Certainly, with access to the outside world, the culture will change. And the mountains and the landscape? They seem immutable, but on close inspection, they too have changed, and grown more than a couple of feet since Nepal first opened her doors to the outside world.

Suspension bridge between Chomrong and Sinuwa

MORE HISTORIC HIKES

Inca Trail to Ingapirca,
Ecuador

OPPOSITE
Great Wall of China, China

Great Wall of China, China

When the "New Seven Wonders of the World" were announced in 2007, it was no surprise that the Great Wall of China made the list. Mostly visited on one-day guided tours, the Great Wall of China is one of the world's most recognizable landmarks. More than 10,000 miles long (experts differ on the exact number), it originally functioned as a fortification to protect China's borders from nomadic tribes to the north. For day hikers, there are many walkable sections close to Beijing. For longer treks, guide services can arrange multiday visits to less-crowded sections of the wall in Jiankou, Mutianyu, Gubeikou, Jinshanling, Simatai, and Huanghuacheng. Guide services also help with logistics and bureaucratic challenges. Note that although the wall was designed to be passable by horsemen, time and weather have degraded the structure so that walking along it can be challenging, with rocky sections and steep ups and downs. Some detours are necessary.

Inca Trail to Ingapirca, Ecuador

If the expense, crowds, and planning challenges put you off the Classic Inca Trail in Peru, the 24-mile three-day Inca Trail to Ingapirca, Ecuador, is a far less-crowded option. It offers a hiking experience through mountainous terrain up to 15,800 feet and the opportunity to camp and trek independently—although a popular way to hike it is with a guide and muleteer. This trek follows part of the Inca Camino Real, which once linked Cuzco and Quito over the Andean *páramo*, with mountain views, glaciers, lagoons, and some Inca ruins you're unlikely to be sharing with other visitors. It ends at the castle complex of Ingapirca, the largest known Inca ruins in Ecuador, which, like Machu Picchu, contain buildings that honor the sun and mark the solstices.

Offa's Dyke Path, England

Some kings build pyramids, some commission statues; the eighth-century Saxon King Offa built a pile of dirt. Offa's Dyke, Britain's longest ancient monument, is an earthwork fortification constructed as a monument to Offa's greatness and as a discouragement to the hostile Welsh Celtic tribes in the west from raiding his kingdom. In the 12th century, it became the border between Welsh nobles and Norman conquerors, who augmented the fortifications with a line of defensive castles. Today, Offa's Dyke Path is a 177-mile English National Walk from Chepstow to Prestatyn. It passes

through a variety of landscapes, including the Black Mountains, the Shropshire Hills, the Eglwyseg moors, and the Clwydian Range. Most hikers take about 12 days for the entire trek.

C&O Canal Towpath, United States

Part of the Potomac Heritage National Scenic Trail, the C&O Canal was the realization of an idea originally proposed by George Washington as a way to open trade routes to the as-yet-unknown west. Built between 1824 and 1850, it operated until 1924. The old towpath is now a 185-mile hiking and biking path, with campsites every few miles. On its way to Cumberland, Maryland, it passes the historic town of Harpers Ferry, West Virginia, site of John Brown's raid, and, just up the hill in neighboring Bolivar, a small Civil War battlefield. Its Paw Paw Tunnel was considered a 19th-century engineering marvel. The towpath starts in Washington, DC, contains a tiny section of the Appalachian Trail, and is the central core of the 800-mile Potomac Heritage National Scenic Trail.

Petra Trek, Jordan

The typical way to visit Petra, the fabled trading city once immortalized as "a rose-red city, half as old as time," is to enter through the famed Siq, a slot canyon that opens to reveal the sculpted majesty of the treasury building hewn into rock by first-century Nabateans. But it is possible to take a five- to nine-day guided trek across the desert via an informal series of donkey paths and roads. Beginning at the Dana Nature Reserve, the trek crosses four climate zones. Entering Petra from the back side—possibly one of the ways ancient traders entered or exited the complex—trekkers come face to face with temples, mausoleums, and tombs, all cut out of the desert rock. The chance to traverse the ancient terrain on foot through the rolling hills and valleys, *sere wadis*, and sandstone cliffs is an opportunity to travel the same lands at the same pace as traders on the ancient Spice Route.

New England Trail, United States

One of the newest of the 11 trails in the US National Scenic Trails System, the 215-mile New England Trail begins at Long Island Sound and traverses Connecticut and Massachusetts, passing 40 towns along the way.

Much of it follows the Mattabesett, Metacomet, and Monadnock Ridges, including old Native American travel ways and ridges and forests where Metacomet, a Native American leader (also known as King Phillip), fought the New England European settlers in one of the deadliest wars in colonial history.

Hadrian's Wall Path, England

In the second century AD, Britannia was the northernmost part of the Roman Empire, and Hadrian's Wall was its effective boundary. Built in 122 AD by the Emperor Hadrian, it served as a defensive line from the North Sea to the Irish Sea. Built of stone, the wall was fortified with a series of ditches and mounds, with castles spaced about five miles apart. Today, what's left of the wall is a World Heritage Site and the most popular tourist attraction in northern England. The Hadrian's Wall Path, one of the English National Walks, follows it for 84 miles from coast to coast past old Roman forts, museums, craft fairs, historic churches, and cozy villages.

OPPOSITE
Offa's Dyke Path, England

C&O Canal Towpath, Maryland, United States

PREVIOUS SPREAD
Petra Trek, Jordan

New England Trail,
Massachusetts (opposite
and right) and
Connecticut (top right),
United States

FOLLOWING SPREAD
Hadrian's Wall Path,
England

CHAPTER 3

PEAK EXPERIENCES

Mountains are the poster children of the hiker's world. We know them as beauty spots, as peak experiences, as challenges. We love them as places for relaxation, rejuvenation, restoration. We crave them as retreats from lives that have become busy, urban, technology centered, crowded, and clangorous. Glaciers, precipices, hundred-mile views: mountains are our escape. • "Mountains seem to answer an increasing imaginative need in the West," wrote Robert Macfarlane in *Mountains of the Mind: Adventures in Reaching the Summit*. "More and more people are discovering a desire for them, and a powerful solace in them. At bottom, mountains, like all wildernesses, challenge our complacent conviction—so easy to lapse into—that the world has been made for humans by humans." • And yet, for most of western history, mountains have been regarded very differently, as dangerous and evil environments to be feared and avoided.

In the heart of Europe, where today comfortable refuges greet weary walkers and hikers scurry up mountain paths in long lines like columns of countless ants, the Alps were once seen as the abode of strange and frightening beasts. Elves lived there, and imps, and goblins. Monsters and demons. And any of them might be prone to mercurial tantrums, throwing avalanches of snow or piles of rocks to immolate villages and destroy crops. Why on earth would anyone in their right mind ever climb a mountain? Such an intrusion could only antagonize the sadistic spirits and the temperamental giants that lived among the rocks and the glaciers and the cold, howling winds.

Thus, Mont Blanc was the "Accursed Mountain." The trendy Swiss ski and film festival town of Les Diablerets was named for the devilish spirits that inhabited its spiky peaks. It was flat-out illegal to climb Mount Pilatus—legendarily (if not historically) known as the resting place of a suicidal Pontius Pilate. Not that anyone was lining up to do so, because who wanted to anger spirits that could push the glaciers forward to swallow the villages at its base? Mont Aiguille was inhabited by angels, Grotte de Sassenage by fairies, and the Col de l'Arzelier by the devil himself. All of these were known facts, as facts were known at the time. So were the dragons, which still exist today, although they have moved from the mountains to the heralds and crests of towns, provinces, and cantons throughout Central Europe.

In Christian Europe, high places were suspect. Wasn't it, after all, a mountain where the devil took Jesus to tempt him? No good could come out of sitting on a summit that commanded a view of creation. All those things we revere today in mountains—the release from order and human constructions, the wildness—were seen as terrifying, untamable, uncivilized. Mountains were loathed by painters, artists, and philosophers, and if you had to travel to mountains, it was best to keep your eyes averted from the horrors around you. If you were lucky, you might be protected at mountain passes by monks, who manned hostels for pilgrims and traders unfortunate enough to have to travel through this dangerous terrain. The tradition of mountain hospitality has a long history. Some of it is rooted in fear.

Elsewhere in the world, mountains were also regarded as the abode of spirits and gods—sometimes

PREVIOUS SPREAD
Everest Base Camp Trek, Nepal

Colorado Trail, Colorado, United States

FOLLOWING SPREAD
Presidential Traverse, New Hampshire, United States

as places of awe; sometimes evil, sometimes not. Unless, of course, one ran afoul of the gods, which was always a possibility. The ancient Greeks set their pantheon of squabbling deities on Mount Olympus, from which the immortals wreaked havoc on the humans below. Inca priests built Machu Picchu at 13,000 feet in the Andes to be closer to the spiritual plane; the Meru people regarded Mount Kenya as the home of God; Buddhists of the Himalaya revered mountains such as Machapuchare in the Annapurna Sanctuary and Mount Kailash in Tibet as so holy that, to this day, it is forbidden to climb them.

Today, we have made a complete about-face, and mountain walking is a booming business, although in the history of humans this is a recent development dating only from the late 18th century. The Enlightenment brought a new curiosity about the world, a rejection of superstition, and a romanticism about nature. In America, a continent was opening up with all its mysteries. And in Europe, the spirit of exploration fueled mountaineering expeditions, many of which were undertaken in the spirit of scientific inquiry. In the western part of the United States, explorers crossed the Rocky Mountains and sent back descriptions of western landscapes that were almost inconceivable to eastern sensibilities.

Many of the major European alpine peaks were first climbed in the early 1800s; by the time the first boot-prints were placed on the Matterhorn in 1865, alpinism had matured into a sport complete with guides, organizations, specialized equipment, and conventions. In 1876, the Appalachian Mountain Club, America's oldest recreation organization, was founded to protect the trails and mountains in the northeastern United States. Recreational trails had already existed here since at least 1819, when Abel Crawford and his son Ethan cleared an eight-and-a-half-mile trail to the summit of Mount Washington. Thought to be the oldest recreational hiking trail in the United States, the Crawford Path leads to the top of a mountain that, with the worst recorded weather in the world, may well have once personified an angry god.

What passed for technical alpinism in those early years would be unrecognizable to the mountaineers of today. Clad in sports coats and woolen sweaters, carrying stout hiking sticks, and wearing footwear that could only be described as inadequate, young men with a sportsmanlike bent and a devil-may-care attitude

somehow managed to scramble to the pinnacles of Western Europe. At the same time that these early mountaineers succumbed to the clarion call of the summits, others were hearing the mountains' more seductive siren songs: walkers seeking respite from the growing industrialization and increasing pressures of urban life found what they were looking for not on the summits, but on trails that wrapped around the high places.

And why not? Not all mountains were howling wastelands with hurricane-force winds and nothing but rocks and ice and the occasional lichen. On countless trails, walkers could head to high places to escape the demanding detritus of everyday life. The mountains, once forbidding and frightening, became first a place of sport and achievement, and then a place of peace.

Around the world, hiking, tramping, trekking, fell-walking, and hillwalking (or in England, prone as ever to polite understatement, simply "walking") began to attract aficionados to the mountains. By the latter part of the 20th century, sleeping outside, which had once been associated with poverty, homelessness, and general disrepute, now indicated the opposite: time for leisure and enough money to pay for outdoor equipment that had become high-tech, specialized, and expensive.

Western culture had banished the demons, elves, and monsters of the high places. Visitors were now enraptured with the changing elevations, where climbing a few thousand feet could put the walker half a world away into an entirely new season or ecosystem. And then there were the bragging rights that came with summiting the high points, whether they be of the county, the state, the province, the range, the country, the continent, or even the world. Mount Everest may be beyond the pale for most flatlanders. But the list of mountains accessible to trekkers is long and magical, including 20,000-foot summits, 18,000-foot passes, and names that have become iconic: the Haute Route, the Presidential Traverse, Mount Kilimanjaro.

We come to the mountains for different reasons: to seek and to find, to exert and to rest, to challenge and reward ourselves, to play, to experience beauty, to stretch our bodies and clear our minds. Or perhaps it is something simpler, and John Muir, as he so often did when it came to mountains, said it best: "The mountains are calling and I must go."

Tongariro Northern Circuit, New Zealand

MOUNT KENYA

Kenya

From a distance, Mount Kenya is deceptively unimpressive. Africa's second-highest peak reaches its elevation of 17,057 feet via a long, sloping ridge with a seemingly gentle profile. At the very center of this gentle rise, a raggedly eroded summit plug pokes straight up, some 1,500 feet above the surrounding scree, which falls away to the gentler slopes. But the mountain's vast base and the horizontality of the equatorial East African landscape dwarfs the summit, at least when seen from afar.

But make no mistake, this is a major mountain. Its twin summits Batian (17,057 feet) and Nelion (17,021 feet) are more than high enough to put snow on the equator year-round. An extinct volcano that last erupted between roughly two and three million years ago, Mount Kenya is thought to have once been higher than Mount Kilimanjaro. But time has had its way, and Mount Kenya now sits a solid 2,000 feet lower than its big brother. Kilimanjaro is unquestionably more famous, certainly more dramatic; its iconic cone rises abruptly from the plains of the Serengeti, instantly recognizable, dominating. In contrast, Mount Kenya emerges gently from the landscape, and from far away; its summit seems like an incidental add-on to the long ridge below. As with gold and silver medals in the Olympics, the difference between highest and second-highest peak on a continent is more than the measured elevation difference; in our imaginations, the gap stretches. Each year, more than twice as many people climb (or attempt to climb) Kilimanjaro as Mount Kenya. One could say they are making a grand mistake.

Up close, there is nothing second place about Mount Kenya. Its volcanic massif contains more than a dozen named peaks, as well as tarns and waterfalls, moraines and glaciers, crags and canyons, and some of the most precipitous and variable scenery in all the

View of Mount Kenya

world's mountains. The wind and snow, the glaciations and eruptions, and that implacable duo of water and time, have sculpted the summit into a vertiginous fantasyland of eroded peaks and gorges. The peaks themselves are the remnants of the volcanic plug; the crater that would once have surrounded the plug has long since eroded away. And to top it all off, East Africa's mountains juxtapose grand height with an equatorial location. The result is a unique environment of vegetation and animal life completely different from that found on other mountains worldwide. Nowhere is this ecosystem more diverse, interesting, and visually striking than on Mount Kenya.

Wildlife native to Mount Kenya includes elephants, cape buffalo, elands, bushbucks, waterbucks, zebras, hyenas, colobus monkeys, white-throated guenons, and, at higher altitudes, the ubiquitous rock hyrax, a marmot-sized mammal that is thought, because of its tiny tusks, to be related to the elephant in some arcane taxonomic way. It is not uncommon to hear buffalo snorting at night, and while walking through the forest, hikers might sometimes see moving, crashing trees that indicate an elephant is in the area. The mountain also has been habitat for lions, leopards, bongos, giant forest hogs, and rhinos, but agricultural use of the surrounding areas has shrunk habitat and pushed most of these animals away. The most likely wildlife sightings are the campsite-dwelling hyraxes, eager to scrounge for the crumbs of a granola bar, and the guenon monkeys, which don't wait for scraps and are perfectly willing to steal your food outright, from your hands, if necessary.

Although the animals are dramatic on Mount Kenya, it is the vegetation that takes center stage. More than 800 species have been recorded, 81 of which are endemic to the mountain. Mountain hikers are accustomed to how altitude changes vegetation. The typical pattern repeats all over the world: mixed deciduous forests give way to conifers, which give way to smaller trees better able to withstand the high winds and stingy soils of the high country. Then, above tree line, shrubs and bushes cede to tundra grasses. Finally only the lichens of the rock and ice zone are left. On Mount Kenya, the same general progression appears, but with unique and dramatic variation: mixed broadleaf forests, gallery forests, bamboo forests that clatter in the wind, fog-shrouded moorlands

filled with tussock grasses, and, unique to the equatorial Afro-Alpine zone, forests of giant groundsels and lobelias, plants so weirdly shaped that Theodor Seuss Geisel (of Dr. Seuss fame) was inspired to create the truffula trees of the children's classic *The Lorax*.

The combination of unique geological features and biodiversity has lead to Mount Kenya's protection under a variety of national and international designations as a Kenya National Park (1949), an International Biosphere Reserve (1978), and a National Reserve (2000). In 1997 it was inscribed as a UNESCO World Heritage Site, described as "one of the most impressive landscapes in Eastern Africa with its rugged glacier-clad

OPPOSITE
Senecio keniodendron along the lower slopes of Mount Kenya

Rock hyraxes along the trail on Mount Kenya

summits, Afro-Alpine moorlands, and diverse forests that illustrate outstanding ecological processes." Today, it is managed by Kenya Wildlife Service.

The local people did not need UNESCO or the Kenya Wildlife Service to tell them about the mountain's importance. To them, Mount Kenya has always been sacred. The Maasai pray that their children be like the mountains. The Kikuyu and Embu build their homes with their doors facing the summit cone and believe that God came down from the sky to live on Mount Kenya, his throne on earth. In Kikuyu legend, Gĩkũyũ, the first man and father of the tribe, was taken to the summit of the mountain by God.

Today, Gĩkũyũ's journey to the mountaintop might be a little different, and he would almost certainly not be alone. Approximately 15,000 people visit the mountain each year, most of whom are attempting to hike the 16,355-foot Point Lenana, known as the trekker's peak because it does not require technical equipment or rock-climbing skills. A multiday round-the-high-peaks circuit allows trekkers with more time to explore the entire summit cone of the mountain, walking at about the 14,000-foot level. And three major approach trails offer an opportunity to traverse the massif from one end to the other, or do a simple up-and-back-down-the-same-way itinerary.

Of the three main routes up the mountain, the Naro Moru Route is the most popular because it offers the quickest route to the summit. Unfortunately for those in a rush, quickest does not mean best: this route is the least scenically interesting because the view of the mountain doesn't change as you ascend the valley in a straight line. Climbing via the Naro Moru route also takes trekkers through the mountain's infamous "vertical bog" where hikers hop from one clump of tussock grass to another, sinking up to their ankles in the mud in between, and wearing themselves out while gaining rather more elevation than is good for them. As a result of the fast ascent, Mount Kenya is known for a disproportionately high percent of the world's cases of AMS (acute mountain sickness) precisely because the Naro Moru Route allows trekkers to reach high elevations faster than they can acclimate to them. Although it is possible to climb the mountain in a long weekend, a four- or five-day itinerary will help avoid altitude sickness.

The Sirimon Route is the gentlest and longest, up the Sirimon Valley, where a resident herd of zebras can sometimes be seen. The Chogoria Route is the most scenically dramatic, as it winds and weaves through a series of rock formations and glacial landscapes, with a constantly changing view of the mountain's many faces. Highlights of the Chogoria Route include Vivienne Falls, the Gorges Valley, and the glimmering lakes at Two Tarn, which are fringed by Afro-Alpine vegetation and mirror the peaks and crags above.

Mount Kenya is one of the highest peaks in the world where hikers without special training and equipment can hike independently. Because of the elevation and conditions, inexperienced hikers might find themselves facing danger, not only from altitude sickness, but also from changing weather conditions, snow blindness, dehydration, hypothermia, and sunburn. Temperatures can range from 90°F to well below freezing, and sudden fog can quickly obscure the treadway, cairns, and other trail markers. A unique twist is the equatorial latitude: because of its location on the equator, Mount Kenya has almost exactly even 12-hour days, with sunrise at 5:30 a.m. and sunset at 5:30 p.m. The difference between the longest day of the year and the shortest day of the year is only one minute. The early falling tropical night can catch hikers unprepared.

Some trekkers hire guides, with or without porters, for the trip. This assistance is worth considering for those without mountain experience. Guides (who should have certification from the Kenya Wildlife Service) can be hired in Chogoria or at Naro Moru River Lodge, where gear can also be rented. Try to time your trip for the dry seasons, particularly January, February, early March, and August.

With its combination of high altitude and low latitude, Mount Kenya is a unique mountain, both dangerous and accessible, stunningly beautiful but with storms that can kill. Some of its character traits will be familiar to any mountain hiker: the fast-changing weather, different vegetation bands as elevation increases, the bite of high thin air, the distinctive austerity of the rock and ice zone. And some of its characteristics are uniquely its own. And like all mountains, what it demands first and most of all is respect.

Trail at the 14,000-foot level on the Mount Kenya Circuit

THE HAUTE ROUTE

France and Switzerland

It would not be an exaggeration to say that recreational mountain hiking was born in the Alps. Once the shroud of medieval superstition was lifted, the mountains exerted an almost magnetic pull on scientists and adventurers alike. One first ascent followed another and then another, the summits falling under human feet like dominoes.

It was a tipping point, of sorts: once begun, the age of alpinism grew almost exponentially. The epicenter of this new alpinism was the region between Mont Blanc, the highest peak in Western Europe, and the Matterhorn, often called the most beautiful mountain in the Alps. Certainly it is a mountain with one of the most recognizable and impressive profiles in the world.

Between the two peaks is a mountain pathway known simply as the Haute Route. The original Haute Route was not a walker's path. First traversed in 1861 by members of the British Alpine Club, it was, and remains, a mountaineering route that starts in the Chamonix Valley, then climbs to a series of high passes and into the snow and ice zone above 10,000 feet. The route can be done on skis in winter, or with alpine skills and technical equipment in summer. It is not a hiking trail.

For walkers, a new route staying below 10,000 feet evolved to fill the growing interest in mountain hiking. This lower version—sometimes called the Walker's Haute Route and sometimes (confusingly) just the Haute Route—roughly parallels the original technical route between Chamonix, France, and Zermatt, Switzerland. A network of secondary trails provides options; the various paths sometimes veer away from each other, but always continue in the same general direction. The result is a network of trails that link two of the world's great centers of alpinism. Walkers traverse, at a lower elevation, the same enormous massif enjoyed by the more technical mountaineers: the greatest concentration of 13,000-foot peaks in the Alps, 10 of the 12 highest peaks in Western Europe, a collection of valleys and villages, alpine meadows and glaciers, and the company of ibex, chamois, marmots, and, of course, the pasturing cattle whose cowbells provide a soundtrack for the walker.

Some of the routes and passes have been used as corridors of transportation since the Middle Ages and even before, when they allowed people from one valley to cross over to the next. Today, the hiking paths are enormously popular, as are the jovial alpine refuges, which are the core of a European hiking culture that is very different from the hiking culture found in North America. While North American mountain hikers seek

View of Mont Blanc across Chamonix Valley, France

OPPOSITE

Ibex along the Haute Route above Zermatt, Switzerland

wilderness and solitary campsites, Europeans tend to congregate in groups and stay in huts. Open from mid-June until sometime in early or mid-September, the huts along the Haute Route offer typical family-style meals complete with beer and wine, sleeping space in communal bunkrooms, and high-country camaraderie. Hikers thus walk unburdened by tents, sleeping pads, sleeping bags, and cooking gear. But the refuges can be crowded and noisy, and they can fill up. On the Haute Route reservations are necessary, although they can usually be booked a day or two in advance using a cell phone or asking a hut manager to radio ahead.

In villages, hikers can choose among the many small inns, hostels, and hotels that cater to mountain travelers. A traverse of the Haute Route can be an independent walk, a guided trip, or a self-guided hike, where arrangements for lodgings and meals are made by a tour company, but hikers walk on their own.

The Walker's Haute Route requires no technical equipment—no ropes, crampons, hardware, or harnesses—though the use of ski poles for balance and support is almost universal, and a sturdy set of legs and lungs is required. Trails are well maintained, with the obvious proviso that the extreme mountain weather and landscape sometimes results in water damage and rockslides. They are also well marked, although a map is necessary to choose among alternate routes and to navigate if fog obscures the route or blazes are otherwise not visible. The route runs approximately 112 miles, crosses 11 high passes, gains more than 12,000 feet of elevation, and takes between nine and 15 days, depending on fitness, route, speed, and hiking style.

The end of the trail offers the option of a two-day traverse of the Europaweg, a 20-mile section of stunning high-country trail that opened in 1997. Note, however, that the Europaweg is frequently closed due to avalanches, storm danger, and the simple fact that the terrain is a bit too fierce for a hiking trail. (When it's closed, alternate lower routes exist.) Some sections require using iron ladders bolted into the mountains; usually, these sections can be bypassed by means of cable cars and chairlifts that run from June through early September, daylight hours only. Some hikers consider this "cheating," but as Appalachian Trail hikers are fond of saying, "Hike your own hike." On a thunderous afternoon when you're already exhausted, a cable car may be a welcome—and sensible—choice.

Regardless of the route, mountain rules apply. While the Alps enjoy rather more temperate summer weather than hikes in such notoriously unsettled climates as Scotland, Patagonia, and New Zealand, snow is possible (even in summer), footing can be treacherous, and thunderstorms are common, particularly in the late afternoons.

The landscape is world class: alpine peaks above; villages below; lakes and glaciers in between, unfolding one after the next. Today, the mountains seem both powerful and welcoming, marked but not destroyed by accessibility and human settlement. As you make your traverse, panting up to passes that may have struck terror in the hearts of villagers who lived in these mountains 500 or 1,000 years ago, it is worth taking a moment to reflect that the views that bring us here were once thought to be the work of the devil. The old French cliché has it that *plus ça change, plus c'est la même chose.* But in this case, everything has changed, and nothing has stayed the same: our human relationship with mountains has undergone a complete metamorphosis in the last 200 years, and nowhere is this more evident than in the place where mountaineering began.

OPPOSITE
Approaching Twara (Stage 12), Haute Route (top); Valais Blackneck goats, Europaweg (Stage 13), Haute Route (bottom)

View from Haute Route toward Plane d'Arolla

FOLLOWING SPREAD
The Matterhorn near Zermatt, Switzerland

THE LONG TRAIL

United States

In 1910, James P. Taylor, an assistant headmaster at a Vermont school, sat on the summit of Stratton Mountain in southern Vermont and conceived of a border-to-border trail that would follow the spine of the Green Mountains. He assembled 23 people to form the Green Mountain Club, whose mission became to "make the Vermont mountains play a larger part in the life of the people by protecting and maintaining the Long Trail system and fostering, through education, the steward-ship of Vermont's hiking trails and mountains."

The new club set abou t trail clearing, starting on Camel's Hump and Mount Mansfield. Within 10 years, they had linked more than 200 miles of trail and a system of trail shelters for overnight use. A decade later, when the idea of a much longer Appalachian Trail was proposed, the Green Mountain Club became involved in that project as well, and the southernmost 100 miles of the Long Trail were incorporated into the Appalachian Trail. The Long Trail was completed in 1930. Today's Long Trail system also includes approximately 175 miles of designated side trails.

The idea suited the era: New England writers of the previous generation, like Thoreau and Emerson, had romanticized Nature with a capital N. With developed trails, mountains were no longer just the realm of expert outdoorsmen; they became the realm of everyman. Recreational walkers arrived in droves.

Vermont's Long Trail—considered America's first long-distance hiking trail—institutionalized the ideas of hiking in the mountains for recreation, for health, and for everyone. Appalachian Trail founder Benton MacKaye also credited it with inspiring his vision of an Appalachian Trail, writing that he himself had sat upon Stratton Mountain musing that, "the Green Mountain Club has already built the 'Long Trail' . . . Here is a

Hiker ascending
Camel's Hump, Long Trail

project that will logically be extended. What the Green Mountains are to Vermont the Appalachians are to the eastern United States. What is suggested, therefore, is a 'long trail' over the full length of the Appalachian skyline, from the highest peak in the north to the highest peak in the south."

As is true on so many trails, numbers—mileage, elevation, and so forth—tell only part of the story. The Long Trail statistics are fairly modest in both mountain and long-distance hiking terms. Today's Long Trail is 272 miles; the trail takes fit hikers about three weeks to hike, sometimes more. The high point is 4,393-foot Mount Mansfield, but short of the rock-capped highest peaks, the mountains here are mostly tree covered, with neither the height nor the rugged first impact of the grand mountains of the West.

Nonetheless, this trail is more difficult than one might think, with a notable absence of the convenience of switchbacks. The Long Trail hiker encounters rocks, roots, mud, wooden puncheons laid over bogs, blackflies in spring, and steep scrambles—sometimes all at the same time. Progress can be slow, sometimes to the tune of a mile an hour. This is especially true in the north, where the Long Trail has some of the most difficult hiking to be found anywhere, its rock scrambles comparable to the famously difficult treadway in the White Mountains or the Mahoosucs.

The trail follows the main ridge of the Green Mountains wherever possible. Starting at its southern end at the Massachusetts border, it climbs most of the range's major summits (some of which are well-known ski areas) including Glastenbury Mountain, Stratton Mountain, Killington Peak, Mount Abraham, Mount Ellen, Camel's Hump, Mount Mansfield, and Jay Peak. The northern terminus, also known as "Journey's End," is at the Canadian border near North Troy, Vermont.

Long Trail along Mount Mansfield

Lower slopes of Piko Peak near Churchill Scott Shelter (left); ladders along forehead of Mount Mansfield (right)

In addition to the peaks and passes, the trail meanders through or around ponds, beaver dams, alpine bogs, streams, waterfalls, and rocky outcroppings, as well as forests of maple, birch, beech, pine, hemlock, spruce, and balsam fir. Wildlife includes black bears, moose, porcupines, beavers, fox, whitetail deer, and peregrine falcons.

The Long Trail can be hiked from late spring through late fall, although parts of it are closed during April and May, usually to prevent erosion damage from snowmelt and mud, and sometimes to protect peregrine nesting sites and alpine flora. In June, the trail is open but as cranky as a person who has been woken too early in the morning: expect mud, blackflies, and mosquitoes. Summer is pleasant, although sometimes quite humid. Many hikers who can arrange their schedules choose September and early October. For those who don't mind colder temperatures, this is prime hiking season, with Vermont's famed autumn colors at their peak. Pack for cold nights, and remember that early season snow at high elevations is possible. In winter, snowshoeing is popular on some sections, but the steep grades and rock scrambling make most of the route impractical for cross-country or backcountry skiing.

The majority of thru-hikers go northbound, taking approximately three weeks to complete the trail. Starting from the Massachusetts border, hikers follow the Appalachian Trail, which is contiguous with the Long Trail for the southernmost 100 miles. It is a good break-in period for the more rugged northern part of the trail.

The Green Mountain Club maintains the Long Trail; it also works to conserve the wilderness character of the Green Mountain region. In the mid-1930s, the club opposed a proposal for a Green Mountain Parkway that would have run along the length of the range. And in the 1950s, the club once again marshaled opposition, this time to a missile communications facility that the US Air Force wanted to build on Mount Mansfield. About 100 core volunteers maintain shelters, build puncheons, install water bars, clear brush, and paint blazes.

But as for making the trail easier? Don't bet on it. Vermonters, it seems, like their trail just the way it is.

Summit of Mount Mansfield,
Long Trail

PRESIDENTIAL TRAVERSE

United States

A sign at the trailhead does not mince words: "STOP. The area ahead has the worst weather in America. Many have died there from exposure, even in the summer. Turn back now if the weather is bad."

In a book that covers the Alps, the Rockies, the Andes, and the Himalaya, 6,288-foot-tall Mount Washington in New Hampshire seems like a junior varsity football wannabe who wandered into the NFL and is ferociously bragging about the time he sacked, well, anyone. Skeptics might justifiably point out that Mount Washington can only lay claim to the worst *recorded* weather in the world: its weather station operates year-round, and there are plenty of places too remote to have recording equipment where the weather is likely far worse. Regardless of such niceties, the numbers are enough to frighten even Himalaya-hardened veterans: a record wind speed of 231 miles per hour, 110 days per year when wind gusts exceed hurricane force, and an average year-round temperature of 27 degrees. The only hikers who aren't scared of those numbers are people who have never been knocked over by gale-force winds or hit by a surprise storm above tree line.

What Mount Washington lacks in bulk, it makes up for in attitude: quite simply, it's a serial killer. More than 150 people have died in the Presidential Range (and the list gets longer every year). Like the cleverest of killers, this one has no pattern. Victims may be novices or experts, and the weapons change from one death to the next: hypothermia, avalanches, ice and rockfall, car accidents, heart attacks, and falls. What is most dangerous about the Presidential Range is its combination of accessibility and unpredictability: most days, the mountains are complacent enough, or at least, not deadly, lulling visitors into a sense of security. But their moods can change quickly. The best defense is good gear, up-to-date information, and respect for the power of these small but fierce peaks.

The native Abenaki did not climb here; they believed Mount Washington's summit belonged to the gods, and quite sensibly stayed away out of respect and fear of offending them. The first European to reach the summit was a 17th-century surveyor and settler named Darby Field. He climbed to show the Abenaki that he was unaffected by their gods; he thought his invulnerability would make the Native Americans more inclined to do business with him on favorable terms. (And indeed, he survived, and went on to negotiate successful land deals.)

Others were not so lucky. Lizzie Bourne was one of the first to die while climbing. In 1885, clad in 45 yards of fabric, including a long skirt, several petticoats, pantaloons, and stockings, the 23-year-old perished within a few hundred feet of the summit house, which was hidden from view by darkness that had fallen too quickly and a swirling fog that obscured the landmarks.

As with Mount Kenya, part of this mountain's danger is its accessibility: a road runs to the top. So does a cog railroad. The Appalachian Trail is blazed right to the summit house, which is built to withstand winds of up to 300 miles an hour, and serves chili and hot coffee. Tourists wander around in lightweight jackets and running shoes, surprised to find themselves shivering when they began their day in balmy temperatures at the base of the mountain. Even backpackers come unprepared, seemingly ignorant that this peak, which lies right in the path of three weather systems, can magnify a run-of-the-mill squall into a mountain monster.

Dangerous, yes, but also iconic. Mount Washington is the tallest mountain in the Northeast, and the Presidential Range offers the region's best sustained above-tree-line hiking experience. The Presidential Traverse cuts through

Hiker ascending
Mount Eisenhower

FOLLOWING SPREAD
Hikers ascending
Mount Monroe

the heart of the White Mountains, and includes a lung-busting 9,000 feet of elevation gain (and loss) in a mere 22 miles as it vaults over the summits of Mounts Madison, Adams, Jefferson, Clay, Washington, Monroe, Franklin, Eisenhower, and Pierce. (Mounts Jackson and Webster aren't considered part of the traverse because Jackson isn't named for the president, and Webster is fewer than 4,000 feet. Hikers can, however, take side trails to them.)

There are several variations of the Presidential Traverse, but the core hike begins at US Route 2 at the northern end of the Presidentials at the Valley Way/Appalachia Trailhead and heads south. Going southbound gets the tough climb of Mount Madison over with when legs and lungs are still fresh. The trail then spends most of its time above tree line until ending at Crawford Notch on Route 302.

This is tough hiking: Appalachian Trail thru-hikers, used to banging out 20 miles a day at a rate of three miles an hour, often see their mileage cut in half in the Whites. This is a good time to remember that in the hiking world, all miles are not created equal. As on the Long Trail, White Mountain trails resemble the New Englanders who built them: tough, direct, and not outwardly friendly. So it seems ironic that this inhospitable terrain was one of the earliest tourist destinations in the United States—developed with the idea of welcoming visitors who hailed from far less challenging climates. The 8.2-mile Crawford Path, which the Presidential Traverse follows for nearly half of its route, was built as a bridle path in 1819 and is the oldest mountain hiking trail in the United States. The first summit house on Mount Washington opened in 1852. The auto road dates from 1861, when it was built as a coach road for Victorians to use in their mountain outings. And the Cog Railway dates from 1869.

The *pièce de résistance* of mountain hospitality in the United States is the Appalachian Mountain Club (AMC) high-mountain hut system, modeled after the alpine refuges in Europe. The eight AMC huts are spread over about 56 miles, approximately a day's walk apart on the Appalachian Trail. Each offers communal sleeping quarters and hearty meals, making the mountains accessible to average hikers without backpacking equipment. The AMC dates from 1876 when a group of gentlemen gathered at the Massachusetts Institute of Technology to found a club devoted to exploring New England's

highest peaks. One of the new club's first projects was to build a hut at Madison Spring.

Working on the hut "croos" (as they are called) is something of a tradition for outdoor-oriented New England college students, who clean rooms, cook food, perform skits on how to fold blankets and make beds, and pack in heavy loads of supplies in old-school wood-framed backpacks that look like medieval torture devices. Other duties include educating visitors about leave-no-trace principles and mountain safety—and sometimes helping rescue those who didn't learn quite enough. Hikers who don't want to stay in the huts can reserve tent space in designated camping areas. There is no unregulated camping above tree line in order to conserve the delicate vegetation in an ecosystem that is unique in the Northeast.

The Presidential Traverse is sometimes done by marathon-level uber-hikers in a long, dangerous day. For mere mortals, it's better attempted as a three-day hike, with overnight stops at the huts at Mount Madison and Lakes of the Clouds. (Some hikers additionally stop at Mizpah Springs, near Route 302 at the southern end of the traverse.) Continuing south from Route 302 on the Appalachian Trail over scenic Franconia Ridge would add two to four more days of tough hiking, including overnights at some combination of the huts at Zealand Falls, Galehead, and Greenleaf.

With or without an extension into the southern White Mountains, a hike of the Presidential Traverse demands effort, flexibility, preparation, and good gear. The reward: an unparalleled opportunity to experience the tundra environment and the magnificent rush of the world above tree line.

Cog railway near summit
of Mount Washington (top);
Star Lake and distant Mount
Washington (bottom)

OPPOSITE
Trail along Mount Moriah

WEST HIGHLAND WAY

 *Scotland*

Glen Etive from Kings
House Hotel

OPPOSITE
Deer at Kings House
Hotel, looking toward
Buachaille Etive Mor and
the mouth of Glen Coe

Scotland's most famed outdoor hiking adventure begins 20 minutes outside Glasgow at a stone obelisk in a pedestrian mall in the town of Milngavie. The first miles showcase all the charms of suburbia: shopping, construction, and parking lots.

But have patience, because the early miles hardly portend what lies ahead. Some 30,000 hikers complete the entire 95-mile West Highland Way every year; another 50,000 or so do shorter segments of it. They aren't here for the shopping.

Conceived in the 1960s, and officially opened in 1980, Scotland's first official long-distance footpath connects the central lowlands of Scotland with the heart of the Scottish Highlands. It earns its reputation among the world's great walks with a combination of loch-shore scenery, desolate north-latitude mountain landscapes, and the chance to take a side trip to the top of Great Britain's highest peak.

The suburban streets near Glasgow soon give way to forested paths as the trail reaches the promisingly named forest of Mugdock. The trail's waymarks, adorned with a Scottish thistle, lead onward, following hiking paths, old military roads, and drovers' paths through scenic glens, over ridges and moors, and past all kinds of bodies of water: sea lochs, freshwater lochs, rivers, and tiny streams. Highlights include the pastoral landscapes beneath the Campsies (the birthplace of Scottish skiing), the serene beauty of Loch Lomond (Scotland's largest lake, measured by surface area), the majestic and temperamental Highlands, expansive Rannoch Moor (an important ecological area), the Devil's Staircase (named for the difficulty of building a road there), historic Glencoe (the site of one of the most notorious slaughters in Scottish history), and Loch Leven (the largest lowland loch in Scotland).

The mountains here are relatively low—the trail goes as low as sea level and rises to a high point of only 1,800 feet. But the trail offers the opportunity to climb Ben Lomond, which, at 3,185 feet, is the southernmost of Scotland's Munros (mountains with elevations of more than 3,000 feet). The trail also passes the base of Ben Nevis, the highest peak not only in Scotland, but in all of the British Isles, a collapsed volcano that rises to 4,409 feet. Regardless of the modest-sounding elevations, the often treeless mountainsides and the

prominence of the mountains looming above expansive valleys give these peaks the feel of much higher mountains. The summit of Ben Nevis is irresistible, a chance to cap the journey with a literal peak experience. But don't expect to be alone: some 100,000 people make the ascent every year. The trail ends at an obelisk in Fort William.

The popularity of the West Highland Way has had both costs and benefits. On the trail, too many boots tromping through too much mud causes erosion. On the other hand, a constant stream of hikers encourages the development of businesses whose services have made the trail accessible to all levels of walkers. With inns spread at regular intervals along the trail, there is no need to carry camping gear, not to mention backpacking food and stoves. There is, however, a need for reservations, as pubs and inns book up during the high season.

The trail is known as an ideal mountain trail for beginning hikers because it stays fairly low yet winds

Sailboat on Loch Leven near the town of Glencoe

OPPOSITE
Cattle along West Highland Way between Milngavie and Drymen

through mountainous terrain, and because it is well marked and easy to follow. Although the majority of hikers do self-guided hikes, guide services are available for those who don't feel confident on their own. In addition, local businesses will book accommodations and arrange to transport baggage from one town to the next. For those who prefer, wild camping is allowed along almost all of the route. With services along the trail, consistent waymarks, and a route that rises high enough for views but not so high as to tempt the thunderstorm gods, the West Highland Way is manageable for fit and determined walkers. Most hikers complete the trail in about a week, walking in a northerly direction to save the drama of the high peaks for last.

Challenges along the trail include that implacable Scottish duo, midges and weather. Midges (small biting flies) begin swarming in May and last well into August. Head nets, clothing that covers the skin, and insect repellent will all help (local pubs sell Skin-so-Soft, which has a reputation for repelling midges). But the best respite comes when it rains, which it does—often. Other challenges include some steep climbs, including a particularly daunting stretch along the shores of Loch Lomond, and exposure to potentially severe wind and weather on some of the highest ridges. May is the most popular month for hiking, but the trail can be hiked spring through fall and even in winter—although only experienced hikers with winter skills and equipment should attempt it.

In June 2010, the West Highland Way was designated as part of the International Appalachian Trail, an ambitious attempt to link long-distance paths in North America and Europe. The network will one day run from southern Florida up to Newfoundland, then jump across the ocean to follow trails through Greenland, Iceland, Scotland, and England, before hopping the channel to Europe and heading south to end—somewhat unbelievably—in the Atlas Mountains of Morocco.

OPPOSITE
Loch Lomond from near the top
of Conic Hill

Bridge of Orchy over the River
Orchy (top); abandoned boot along
West Highland Way (bottom)

THE GR20

France

The *maquis*. The word has traveled some: it was used as a name for French Resistance fighters who hid in the bush, then it was appropriated in the Star Wars mythos. But it comes from the Mediterranean island of Corsica, and it refers to the spiky, prickly, scrubby brush that grows wild over the dry mountains, encroaching on trails, grabbing at hikers' ankles, catching on fire, and generally making a nuisance of itself. On Corsica, famed for long feuds and high passions, *maquis* in the mountains created an obstacle between someone who wanted to hide and someone who wanted to find him.

The smell is a combination of the kind of prickly dry plants that belong in a potpourri bowl: rosemary, thyme, juniper, lavender, heather, myrtle, marjoram, and more. All them are similarly pungent, pugnacious herbs that eschew water—who needs it? But though they are tough plants suitable for a tough land, their scent is seductive. It wafts across the island on the sere winds of mountains that poke 9,000 feet up from the sea.

Corsica's high point is 9,978-foot Monte Cinto; 20 other peaks rise above 6,562 feet (2,000 meters), and two-thirds of the landscape is mountainous. It earns an easy place on the list of the world's most mountainous islands. Craggy, steep sloped, rocky, and covered with *maquis*, this is an unforgiving place, famed for producing a culture of people as tough as their land. Like a local boy named Napoleon Buonaparte.

The entire island of Corsica is only 113 miles long. The GR20 goes from one end to the other—112 miles in all. The vertical elevation gained (and lost) is about 35,000 feet. Each day's walk averages about 2,500 feet of climbing and descending. It is said to be the most difficult walk in Europe.

The entire hike takes about 15 days, but in those two weeks, the GR20 presents all the difficulties of

Capitello Lake, GR20

FOLLOWING SPREAD
Cascade des Anglais
waterfall, GR20

mountain hiking along with most of the challenges of desert hiking. Daytime temperatures are high; there is little water and even less shade. Unstable trails often seem to hug the very edge of precipices that drop away a thousand feet or more. This may be a suitable habitat for eagles and hawks, or perhaps for the mouflon, the native mountain sheep. For hikers laboring under the weight of backpacks, it is challenging and sometimes terrifying, with some sections requiring rock scrambling and a few even requiring the aid of via ferrata–like chains and cables bolted into the rock. Guidebooks warn that "perfect" fitness is required. Hikers recovering at mountain refuges at the end of weary days often concur that having a little more perfection in the fitness department might not have been a bad idea.

None of which dissuades hikers. Some are drawn by the challenge, others by the trail's reputation for scenic drama. Some even attempt the trail in winter: from February to April, experienced backcountry skiers with a guide can attempt the l'Alta Strada, a winter variant of the GR20 in the northern part of the island. It is also sometimes possible for experienced hikers with appropriate mountaineering and snow gear to hike between November and January and between May and June, although this requires skill and planning. Snow and adverse weather can create dangerous conditions, and the huts, while open for shelter, provide no off-season services or food.

For most hikers, the best time to tackle the traverse is either in late June or early September: in both time frames, most of the huts are open with full services, the weather is not as oppressively hot as it is in midsummer, and the trails are less crowded.

Perhaps because of the higher elevations and rockier trail, the northern part is often described as more difficult. (It is also usually described as more beautiful.) Nonetheless, of those attempting the entire trail, most hike north to south. Hikers starting from the south usually find the terrain more gentle but the climate more challenging: temperatures along the trail's lower southern section are quite a bit hotter than they are in the higher north.

The trail is usually broken into two sections, from Calenzana to Vizzavona in the north and from Vizzavona to Conca in the south. The train station midway at Vizzavona makes for a convenient embarkation

and disembarkation point for those doing half the trail. On the trail, mountain refuges (with meals and mattresses available, but reservations recommended) are spaced about a day's walk apart. Camping is permitted near the refuges, but not elsewhere. The refuges offer dorm-style accommodations for 25 to 50 people and meals at reasonable prices.

The mountains of Corsica are crisscrossed by a network of trails. Hikers wanting to experience the mountainous interior of Corsica without undertaking the sometimes extreme challenges of the GR20 can try one of several other less arduous routes: the Tra Mare e Monti crosses the GR20 in the north near Calenzana; the Mare a Mare Nord crosses the GR20 at Col de Vergio; and the Mare a Mare Centre takes a central route and crosses at the Col de Laparo.

But for those who have the time and stamina, the GR20 is worth the effort: it is a true sky-island environment, an alpine geography dumped in the middle of the famously blue Mediterranean. It compresses a great deal of ecological variety, topography, and scenery into a relatively short two-week hike, from dryland chaparral to glacial lakes, grassy meadows, crags, and peaks, along with opportunities to take side trails to some of the highest peaks in Corsica, including Mount Cinto, the island's high point.

Not to mention the endless hillsides of *maquis*, the sweet and pungent smell of which might linger in your memory long after you leave the island. In exile on the island of Elba some 50 miles away, Napoleon said that when the *maquis* was burning, he could smell it on the winds. He said it carried memories of home and made him weep.

Spasimata Valley, GR20

COLORADO TRAIL

United States

Take a landscape of 14,000-foot peaks and add insummer thunderstorms, snowfields, and multi-thousand-foot climbs. Then try to create a 500-mile trail that is accessible not only to super-fit long-distance hikers, but to ordinary walkers: folks out for a weekend, families, recreational hikers not accustomed to having arguments with mountain gods intent on hurling lightning bolts directly at them from the sky.

That is the challenge that faced trail visionaries in the early 1970s as they contemplated developing a state-wide trail in Colorado. The numbers are downright intimidating: the Colorado Trail runs 486 miles from Denver to Durango through six wilderness areas, six national forests, and eight mountain ranges. It reaches its high point of 13,271 feet just below 13,334-foot Coney Summit. The average elevation of the trail is more than 10,000 feet, with a total elevation gain of almost 90,000 feet. All this on a trail where the intent was to provide outdoor recreation for everyman. Through *those* mountains. In *that* terrain.

Conceived by regional foresters Bill Lucas and Merrill Hastings of *Colorado Magazine*, the Colorado Trail was formed as a grassroots effort, led in large part by trail advocate Gudy Gaskill. The founders never lost their populist mission. The trail thus has a continually improving system of switchbacks, bridges, and "reassurance" trail markings (they are placed not to show the route, but to reassure hikers that they are still on the route). Perhaps even more important, it tries to avoid, as much as possible, some of the serious dangers of mountain travel, such as the daily summer thunderstorms that can trap hikers on high exposed ridges with nowhere to turn for shelter. For hikers addicted to the stark, harsh world above tree line, these routing choices can be frustrating. But there is no question that they are sensible.

Sliderock Ridge,
Colorado Trail

To make backpacking accessible to those who might struggle with a full pack, the Colorado Trail Foundation also organizes supported group hikes with vans that meet hikers at the end of the day with supplies and camping equipment. The trail is mostly nonmotorized, but it is a shared-use path, open to whatever uses land-management regulations allow: all of the trail is open to hikers and stock users; nonwilderness areas are open to mountain bikes. In wilderness sections, where bicycles are not permitted, the Colorado Trail Foundation provides maps and suggests alternate legal routes. The presence of cyclists, hikers, and livestock on the trail is firmly rooted in the trail's tradition, but it can create conflict. Bicycle use, in particular, can erode certain types of trail, and all three user groups are sometimes guilty of not following right-of-way protocols. Nonetheless, the groups seem to coexist rather more amicably here than on some other trails.

For all the talk of accessibility, there are plenty of places where the trail simply cannot be tamed. Especially in wilderness areas, the lay of the mountains sometimes forces the trail to stay above tree line or to traverse open alpine meadows, sometimes for miles at a time. There simply isn't anywhere else to go.

This is not a bad thing: while it may be sensible to avoid the highest passes, it is the high, open landscapes that give this trail its reputation. Hikers come here for the mountains. True, looking out at a sea of peaks that extends to the far horizon can be overwhelming to a hiker who suddenly realizes that hiking the Colorado Trail means walking over and through that vast, seemingly unlimited mountain landscape. Overwhelming or

Colorado Trail
along Mount Shavano

OPPOSITE
Cascade Creek,
Colorado Trail

not, and despite the dangers and physical challenges, the trail's high, wild sections will always be its poster children. They attract long-distance hikers and wilderness lovers like moths to a flame.

Because of the high mountain landscape, the season for hiking the Colorado Trail is necessarily short, extending (depending on the annual snowfall) from late June through early September. In some years, the lower sections near Denver may be accessible as early as April. In high snow years, the higher elevations may be snowbound well into July. Most end-to-enders start in Denver and head west, which allows them to begin earlier in the season. Also, a westbound hike gives hikers a bit more breaking-in time before facing the challenges of the heart of the Rockies. The typical thru-hike takes five or six weeks, with an average of about 40 days.

The Colorado Trail is contiguous with the Continental Divide Trail (which runs 3,100 miles from Mexico to Canada) for about 234 miles starting in the San Juan Mountains. A new 80-mile section of trail—the Western Collegiate Peaks—has recently been added to the Colorado Trail system as an alternate. This is the preferred route for the Continental Divide Trail, but it is now part of the Colorado Trail system as well. Linking the traditional Colorado Trail segment with this new Continental Divide segment makes for a 160-mile loop through the Collegiate Peaks.

It is interesting to consider that from the earliest days of settlement and trade, crossing the Continental Divide has been the enduring problem of Colorado. Railroad builders, silver miners, road builders, fur traders, water planners: all have had to face the problem of crossing the great monolith of the Divide. Enormous coffers of funds, machinery, and manpower were expended to meet the challenge. How remarkable is it, then, that a group of trail builders, often using hand tools, has managed to carve out a 500-mile route through the heart of the Rockies, accessible to a wide range of outdoor users? The Colorado Trail Foundation has made difficult routing decisions; accommodated mountain bikes, stock users, and hikers; created a system of van-supported hikes that makes the trail more accessible; and worked within the regulations of a variety of multiple-use lands, forests, and wilderness areas. Added together, the mere fact of the Colorado Trail is something little short of a miracle.

Pine Creek and Mount Oxford, Colorado Trail

WONDERLAND TRAIL

United States

Mount Rainier looms over the landscape of southwestern Washington like some out-of-scale geological incarnation of Godzilla. At 14,411 feet, it is the highest peak in Washington State and the highest peak in the Cascades, but the numbers don't adequately describe its dominance. Like a whale shark next to a school of minnows or a sequoia in a greenhouse, it seems completely out of scale, ridiculously bigger than anything around it.

The explanation is the term *prominence*. Mount Rainier has the highest prominence—13,211 feet—of any peak in the contiguous United States. In the language of mountains, vertical prominence is a measurement of height in relation to the surrounding landscape. A 5,000-foot mountain looming over a 1,000-foot plain has a 4,000-foot prominence, more than a 14,000-foot mountain rising above a jumble of 12,000-foot peaks. Other factors, of course, enter the equation when discussing the nature of mountains: latitude, elevation, weather patterns, and technical difficulties. For example, Mount Rainier's vertical prominence is slightly greater than that of the Himalayan giant K2, but we can't forget that K2 pokes its head into the oxygen-deprived 26,000-foot death zone. Nonetheless, by any measure, Mount Rainier is impressive. In the United States, only Denali (Alaska) and Mauna Kea (Hawaii) have a greater vertical prominence.

Mount Rainier is also one of the world's most potentially dangerous volcanoes. It erupted several times in the 19th century—merely yesterday by the standards of geological processes. An episodically active stratovolcano, it is one of only 16 volcanoes on the so-called Decade Volcanoes list maintained by the International Association of Volcanology and Chemistry of the Earth's Interior. The list identifies volcanoes thought to be especially destructive because of their history of

cataclysmic eruptions and their proximity to major population centers. On Mount Rainier, that damage includes the possibility of unleashing volcanic ash, lava flows, pyroclastic flows (avalanches of intensely hot rock and volcanic gases), and lahars (torrents of meltwater containing loose rock, boulders, and slurries of mud) that could travel all the way to Puget Sound.

For Washingtonians, living next door to Mount Rainier is a little like having Godzilla peering at you over the backyard fence. No matter: the mountain is one of Washington's most beloved and recognizable landscapes. Its profile appears on license plates, on postage stamps, on the state quarter, on postcards, and on the covers of guidebooks about Seattle. Its eponymous national park—the fifth park in the US national parks system—attracts nearly two million visitors annually. Only a few hundred attempt to walk around the entire mountain on the Wonderland Trail, a 93-mile national recreation trail that circles the mountain and boasts its own superlatives and extremes.

Weather is one of those extremes: Paradise, a major gateway to the park at 5,420 feet, annually receives an average of 641 inches of snowfall, one of the highest annual snowfall measurements on earth. For hikers, this means that snow often covers the trail, especially at the higher elevations, well into July. Lying entirely within Rainier National Park, the Wonderland Trail is also noteworthy for constant ups and downs. It rises and falls 22,000 vertical feet as it climbs to sometimes snow-covered ridges, then descends to cross the scores of streams and rivers that drain the mountain's 25 named glaciers. Suspension bridges, rocks and boulders, and primitive log planks can make the crossings easier—if they haven't been washed away by meltwater, storms, and flooding. Late summer, after the snowmelt and

Cowlitz Divide and Mount Adams, Wonderland Trail

mosquitoes have abated, is the sweet spot with generally dry weather. But mountain rules apply: storms can roll in off the Pacific Ocean at any time of year. At some point in September, the weather turns wet.

The constantly shifting elevations are a challenge, but they create one of the great attractions of the Wonderland Trail: the experience of constantly changing ecosystems. On a daily basis, lowland forests alternate with subalpine meadows filled with gentians, monkey-flowers, and lupine. Waterfalls cascade along the streams, and the trail opens up to give frequent views of the mountain from all angles. Animals sighted will most likely include marmots and pikas, with the possibility of mountain lions, bobcats, red foxes, coyotes, black bears, raccoons, skunks, weasels, deer, elk, and mountain goats.

Place names like Eagle's Roost, Paradise, and Summerhaven provide obvious clues to the trail's exploding popularity. Although only a small number of hikers attempt the entire trail, many thousands of visitors do shorter sections, and in recent years, backpacking permits, which are assigned by a lottery system, have become increasingly difficult to come by. Reservations open for the season on March 15 and usually quickly sell out, although some slots are held for walk-in reservations.

In the middle of the trail, always looming, is Mount Rainier itself, its glaciers shimmering, blindingly white. This is a mountain whose summit is firmly reserved for climbers, not hikers: even the easiest route requires ropes, crampons, an ice axe, a helmet, a harness, and a companion who knows the way (or better yet, a guide). Some 11,000 hopefuls attempt to climb the mountain each year; more than 50 percent do not make it to the summit, usually due to exhaustion or bad weather.

Some hiker-climbers who have done both the Wonderland Trail and the summit climb say that the trail is the more ambitious of the two undertakings. Climbing Mount Rainier involves 9,000 feet of gain and loss, and is over in two very long days. Walking around the mountain is an almost 100-mile marathon with nearly three times the elevation gain, and takes 10 to 14 days. Neither is for the faint of heart. But both hikes give an up-close-and-personal experience of a mountain that is a beloved and enduring symbol of the Pacific Northwest.

Moonrise above Indian Bar, Wonderland Trail

FOLLOWING SPREAD
Hikers along Wonderland Trail above Indian Bar

MORE PEAK EXPERIENCES

Mount Toubkal, Morocco

Mint tea in the shade of a Berber village. Views into the Sahara Desert. The occasional encounter with a camel. Climbing 13,671-foot Jebel Toubkal is not your everyday mountain experience. The climb itself is relatively simple, especially if you do a quick up and down to the summit. But another option is to combine the climb with a 45-mile trek around the mountain. The Atlas Mountains are the longest range in Africa, extending for some 1,600 miles across North Africa. The High Atlas subrange combines surprisingly green valleys with stark, sere mountainsides. The hiking is not technical, but rocky climbs can be challenging, and some long days make this a suitable trek for fit hikers. The circuit takes four to six days, with camping or accommodations in village guesthouses. Note: yes, it's Morocco, but Jebel Toubkal is nearly 14,000 feet, so if you climb it in winter, be prepared to use an ice axe and crampons. The summer season can be brutally hot, leaving autumn (September through November) and spring (March through May) as the best times for trekking. Summit views include a panorama of the High Atlas Mountains; looking south, you'll see the Jebel Sahro range and the Sahara.

Mount Fuji, Japan

An astonishing 300,000 people climb Japan's highest peak every year—most of them in July and August, meaning that this is one crowded mountain. The 12,389-foot peak on Honshu Island is an active stratovolcano that last erupted in 1707–08. A World Heritage Site, its often snowcapped symmetrical cone is an iconic sight for Japanese and visitors to Japan. The climb is usually done as a two-day trek with a typical alpine start (in the middle of the night) in order to arrive at the summit by goraikō, "arrival of light." There are a number of mountain huts where hikers can rest or stay overnight. Along the way, you'll notice huge switchbacks and retaining walls, designed to try to keep the highly erodible volcanic soil and rock from falling apart under the impact of thousands of hiking boots a day. With the enormous crowds, this is as much a cultural experience as a mountain experience. Two routes—the Subashiri and Gotemba—are unpopular for climbers due to the deep slip-slidey ash, but they offer a unique and fun opportunity for fit hikers with good balance to run and slide down from the summit. (Wear a face mask to keep the dust out of your lungs, and gaiters to keep the sand and ash out of your boots.)

Mount Toubkal, Morocco

OPPOSITE
Mount Fuji, Japan

Mount Kilimanjaro, Tanzania

Coca-Cola route or whiskey route? These are the two top choices for the 35,000 hikers who try to summit Kilimanjaro, Africa's 19,341-foot high point, each year. The five-day Marangu Route (nicknamed the "Coca-Cola route" because of the soft drinks available along the way) is the most popular, but it is also the shortest, giving little time for acclimatization; more than half the climbers on the Marangu Route turn back, usually because of altitude sickness or related exhaustion. The six- to eight-day Machame Route (called the "whiskey route" because it is said to drive the guides and porters to drink) is longer and requires camping, but it has more scenic variety and gives hikers more time to acclimate. Several other longer routes are also options. No special skills or equipment are needed to reach the summit, but all hikers must use a licensed guide service. On summit day, prepare to start hiking in the middle of the night to be at the summit in time to see the sun rise over the Serengeti.

Everest Base Camp Trek, Nepal

The highest mountain in the world has a cachet that extends even to mere trekkers who only want to reach its base. The base camp trek from the Nepal side of the mountain takes hikers into the heart of Sherpa culture in the Sol Khumbu region. While the 2015 earthquake damaged part of the trail, the people of the Khumbu region depend on the trekking route for their own transportation of food and other items, as well as income from trekkers. As a result, locals have been quick to develop alternate paths around stretches of trail destroyed by landslides, and trekker income is helping them rebuild. From the airfield at Lukla, the walk to base camp and back can take anywhere from 12 to 20 days. Plan for some easy days at the start, because altitude sickness can be a problem if you fly into Lukla (elevation 9,383 feet) and then climb too high too quickly. You can also extend the trek by taking the traditional route, starting at Jiri and walking an additional five days to Lukla (you'll also gain an additional 30,000 feet of elevation). The advantage is you see a completely different environment and will enjoy much more solitude: only about one percent of the 30,000 Everest Base Camp trekkers still do the walk from Jiri. Either way, this is one of the world's best-known treks, and the views of the world's highest mountain do not disappoint.

Mount Kilimanjaro, Tanzania

FOLLOWING SPREAD
Everest Base Camp Trek,
Nepal

Tongariro Northern Circuit, New Zealand

A volcanic landscape that is still active, miles of lava fields, steaming vents, and lakes whose vivid turquoise waters seem to vibrate against dark volcanic rock that looks as if it was ejected just yesterday: the 31-mile Tongariro Northern Circuit is one of the most unusual mountain hikes in the world. One of the highlights is the tephra-covered volcano Mount Ngauruhoe, an active stratovolcano that erupted 45 times in the 20th century, most recently in 1974. (Those familiar with *The Lord of the Rings* might recognize it as Mount Doom.) Hikers will have the chance to climb the almost perfect volcanic cylinder and slide back down the loose tephra. (Wear gaiters or you'll have boots full of rock.) The trek takes most hikers three or four days. The one-day Tongariro Alpine Crossing is an abridged version of this trek, going past the Emerald Lakes and Ngauruhoe, although day trekkers usually don't have time to climb. For trekkers on the full circuit, four mountain huts provide shelter. The Tongariro Northern Circuit is one of New Zealand's Great Walks.

Pennine Way, England

In 1932, 500 walkers committed an act of mass trespass on what was ultimately to become the first stretch of the Pennine Way. They were demonstrating for the right to enjoy the open countryside. Today, the Pennine Way is one of England's best-known trails. It is also considered one of the toughest, following the height of land that is Central England's backbone. The 268-mile path begins in Edale, in the northern Derbyshire Peak District and ends at Kirk Yetholm, just inside the Scottish border. In between, it passes through the Yorkshire Dales, the North Pennines, and Northumberland National Park, intersecting the Coast to Coast Walk. The Pennine Way shares a bit of its ethos with the Appalachian Trail, which was its role model: when the idea was first introduced in 1935, it was inspired by the belief that struggling industrial workers needed an outdoor resource to escape to. Following everything from old drovers' trails to Roman roads, the route today crosses open moors and challenging mountains where the weather can change on a dime. An estimated 150,000 people use the Pennine Way each year; about 3,500 hike the entire length.

Tongariro Northern Circuit,
New Zealand

FOLLOWING SPREAD
Pennine Way, England

CHAPTER 4

To WALK *in* WILDERNESS

"Wilderness is a dark and dismal place where all manner of wild beasts dash about uncooked." • This quotation, attributed to an anonymous Virginia settler in the early 1600s, may be apocryphal, but it is typical of the attitude of the era. The mountains of Europe were bad enough, but at least they were dotted with villages and paths and the occasional refuge. The wildernesses of America were far worse, containing not only mountains, but also large wild beasts, endless miles of impenetrable forest, and no towns to provide shelter from the great wild open. Not to mention the Native Americans, who were as incomprehensible to the new arrivals as the wilderness itself. • If walking for recreation is a relatively modern idea in human history, then hiking in wilderness for fun and leisure is revolutionary. But it was a progression that followed quite naturally from the birth of alpinism in Europe. When the same spirit of discovery and inquiry was applied

in 19th-century America, it fell on an entirely different landscape: not mountains with pretty villages at their bases, but a whole unsettled and unknown continent.

This exploration found an immediate emotional resonance, a connection with the zeitgeist of romanticism and transcendentalism, which embraced the uncontrollable and the natural. Wild places were still potentially dangerous and unpredictable, but in the new worldview, that was something to be explored, not avoided. Old maps designated unknown lands at the margins with fanciful drawings of mythical beasts and the warning that "here there be dragons." In the brave new world of 19th-century romantics, the metaphorical dragons of wilderness were to be approached, studied, exploited, appreciated—and, as time went on, maybe even protected.

Sometimes, the dragons roared: Henry David Thoreau's account of his emotional, almost hysterical encounter with a storm on Maine's Katahdin has something of the mythic about it, but it also seems a turning point in our relationship as a culture with wilderness. His encounter with all-powerful Nature with a capital "N" may have been frightening and overwhelming, but it was also life-changing, as mind-altering in its day as psychedelic drugs would be a hundred years later. Thoreau was not only shaken by his encounter with wilderness, he was fascinated by it.

Not all encounters had to be soul-shattering: to the contrary, the literature of the 19th century contains some of the first writing about walking in nature, which was fast being perceived as an antidote to the stresses of civilization. William Wordsworth wrote his poem "Tintern Abbey" after visiting the Wye Valley during a walking tour of Wales; John Keats walked through Scotland, Ireland, and the Lake District; Robert Louis Stevenson trekked through the French region of Cévennes with a donkey. A new form of recreational travel—and a new genre of travel writing—was born.

Over the next century, the relationship between humans and wilderness changed, then changed again. While Thoreau struggled with wilderness, John Muir flowed with it. Theodore Roosevelt sought to dominate it, Benton MacKaye (father of the Appalachian Trail) conceived it as a healing retreat. Aldo Leopold attempted to define it, and of course industry—mining, logging, drilling, and ranching—tried to exploit it.

And then, in the 1960s, two more seminal changes occurred: the Wilderness Act of 1964 protected wilderness. And the rest of us discovered it. The United States was the first country in the world to define and designate wilderness areas through law. It took 60 drafts and eight years, but when the Wilderness Act was passed by the US Congress, it permanently protected some of the most natural and undisturbed places in America.

Prior to the Wilderness Act, most of America's public lands were managed for two broad purposes: commercial use and recreation. National forests were managed in large part for the commercial production of timber as well as for grazing and mining. National parks were managed for recreation. Now we had another category,

defined by law as land that "generally appears to have been affected primarily by the forces of nature, with the imprint of man's work substantially unnoticeable [and] has outstanding opportunities for solitude or a primitive and unconfined type of recreation." A wilderness, the law said, was "an area where the earth and its community of life are untrammeled by man." It would be "devoted to the public purposes of recreation, scenic, scientific, educational, conservation and historic use."

As ancient as the fact of wilderness is, that definition of it is an entirely modern construct that lies in opposition to most land use in history. It separates humans from land, and puts wilderness areas off-limits to development, industry, or any other use that would

John Muir Trail,
California, United States

compromise their ecosystem and character. With that revolutionary idea, the Wilderness Act became one of the most successful US environmental laws: it was passed by an almost unanimous vote, has lasted for more than 60 years without substantial amendment, and has inspired similar legislation in other countries.

However, other countries with different landscapes, population densities, natural resources, and historic patterns of land use have necessarily diverged in how they interpret the idea of wilderness. In some regions, wildernesses are managed in tandem with human uses, including settled towns and traditional nomadic communities. According to *Wilderness: Earth's Last Wild Places*, a study carried out by Conservation International, 46 percent of the world's land mass is wilderness, most of which is quite logically found in the least densely settled parts of the globe: the tundra, the taiga, the Amazonian rain forest, the Tibetan Plateau, the Australian outback, and deserts such as the Sahara and the Gobi. Some of these regions are suitable for hiking, but many certainly are not—at least, not for average vacationers with limited experience in extreme environments and two weeks of vacation time.

The international trails in this chapter were chosen from those wilderness areas that are suitable for and accessible to hikers. They are not, however, necessarily managed the same way as the wilderness trails in the United States.

In Patagonia, at the southern tip of South America, the far southern latitude and high elevations combine to create a place that has never been densely settled and retains much of its wild character simply due to inaccessibility, harsh terrain, and foul weather. The opposite is true in the Pyrenees Mountains of France and Spain, where people have lived in the valleys between the high peaks for centuries. Despite the presence of towns, villages, and farms, this is one of Western Europe's biggest remaining wild areas south of the Arctic. It is also one of the last places with large enough tracts of unsettled wild lands to support a tiny remnant population of the endangered European brown bear. In Newfoundland, along the Long Range Traverse, we find a trail that is so wild, remote, and unmarked that hikers are required to carry locator beacons.

Aldo Leopold defined wilderness as a place where you could take a two-week pack trip and not cross your own tracks. But it is more than that. Wilderness is not merely the absence of intrusions—development, commerce, buildings—it is also the presence of something ineffable: a silence that can be perceived, a sense of space, a connection with the primeval, and a realization that visitors must, by the very definition of wilderness, be self-reliant.

Today's wilderness maps say nothing about dragons. But as we walk away from civilization, watching the bars slowly drain away from our mobile communication devices, we may well feel that we are walking off the edge of the known world. Indeed, that is the gift of wilderness: not just climbing a mountain, or going for a hike, but experiencing the other side of the known horizon. Leaving behind our tamed, mechanized, and familiar home landscape, we step off the edge into the unknown—to experience, wonder at, and, for a time, live with those dragons of our imagination.

Pyrenees High Route, Spain

181

JOHN MUIR TRAIL

United States

In 1868, a 29-year-old man named John Muir arrived in San Francisco, California, and asked directions to anyplace wild. Pointed in the direction of the Sierra Mountains, he headed east to Yosemite Valley, where he found what he was looking for.

"It seemed to me that the Sierra should be called, not the Nevada or Snowy Range, but the Range of Light," he later wrote. "And after ten years of wandering and wondering in the heart of it, rejoicing in its glorious floods of light, the white beams of the morning streaming through the passes, the noonday radiance on the crystal rocks, the flush of the alpenglow, and the irised spray of countless waterfalls, it still seems above all others the Range of Light." Muir's quest for a wild place in which to explore and get lost may seem quite ordinary to our generation. But it was not quite so common in his time. Only half a century earlier, the West was largely unexplored and almost totally unknown. The idea that someone would choose to take a vacation in the rugged outdoors was still new—and unimaginable for most.

Muir was born in 1838; in his lifetime, the barriers between humans and wilderness collapsed like a house of cards. New Hampshire's Mount Washington opened a summit house, trails, a cog railway, and a road, becoming America's first mountain tourist attraction. Emigrants flooded across a wild continent that had until recently been almost entirely unknown to all but Native Americans. By the end of the century, lands that were once wilderness were being logged, ranched, mined, tamed, exploited, and polluted, and the first voices began to be raised about the need to protect them from overuse and ultimate destruction.

One of the most forceful and eloquent of those voices was that of John Muir. Born in Scotland, but raised in Wisconsin, Muir journeyed in Alaska and

Kearsarge Lake Pinnacles, Kings Canyon National Park

in Washington; he walked a thousand miles from Indianapolis, Indiana, to the Gulf of Mexico. He sailed to Cuba, and later to Panama, and traveled through Australia, South America, Africa, Europe, China, and Japan. But he is most firmly and permanently associated with California, in particular with the High Sierra—his "Range of Light."

His love affair with the High Sierra began with that first visit to Yosemite; it continued as he returned to work there as a shepherd. His book, *My First Summer in the Sierra*, a classic in wilderness literature, recounts his first impressions and experiences, which led to a change of heart about the sheep he had protected so conscientiously during those first years. "Hoofed locusts," he called them, after seeing the damage intensive grazing did to the fragile grasses and soils of the mountains. Muir became instrumental in the drive to protect Yosemite, which was designated as a national park in 1890. He was also a founder of the Sierra Club in 1892.

Muir did not, however, conceive of the idea of the eponymous hiking trail that runs the length of the High Sierra from Yosemite Valley to the top of Mount Whitney "Father of the trail" honors belong to Theodore Solomons, whose namesake trail (now seldom used) roughly parallels the John Muir Trail at a lower elevation to the west. According to the Pacific Crest Trail Association, Solomons related that "the idea of a crest-parallel trail came to me one day while herding my uncle's cattle in an immense unfenced alfalfa field near Fresno. It was 1884 and I was 14." In 1915, the Sierra Club received $10,000 from the California legislature to begin construction of the John Muir Trail. Twenty-three years later—100 years after Muir's birth—the trail was completed.

Usually abbreviated as the JMT, the John Muir Trail goes through the John Muir and Ansel Adams Wildernesses, as well as Yosemite and Sequoia and Kings Canyon National Parks—one of the world's classic mountain wilderness landscapes. Added together, these areas form one of the largest protected wilderness complexes in the contiguous 48 states.

The trail's northern terminus is the unwilderness-like Yosemite Valley, with its paved roads, campgrounds, cabins, hotels, restaurants, and even a jail for miscreant recreationists. The southern terminus is atop Mount Whitney, the highest peak in the contiguous 48 states at

Vernal Falls,
Yosemite National Park

FOLLOWING SPREAD
Upper Basin
near Mather Pass

14,494 feet. (From this unlikely trail terminus, it is still an 11-mile hike down to the Whitney Portal Trailhead on the eastern slope of the Sierra near the town of Lone Pine.) For 170 of its 211 miles, the John Muir Trail is contiguous with the Pacific Crest Trail. They meet on the western side of Mount Whitney and, with the exception of a brief stretch near Reds Meadow, share the same path until they split for good near Tuolumne Meadows in Yosemite National Park.

Those 211 miles between Yosemite Valley and the summit of Mount Whitney traverse some of America's most isolated mountain landscapes. From Mount Whitney to Devil's Postpile National Monument, the hiker does not come near a road. There are no power lines, no cell phone towers, no stores, no hotels; only shimmering lakes, dramatic canyons, granite cliffs, crystal-clear streams, high passes, and even higher mountains. Hikers who want to resupply must factor in taking side trails that lead either to not-so-nearby towns or to off-trail wilderness lodges.

While the trail is usually obvious to see (except when covered with snow) and well maintained, the hiking is not easy. Wilderness, you remember, means no human intrusions, and that includes stores where hikers can resupply. The lack of on-trail resupply options between Mount Whitney and Reds Meadow makes for difficult logistics and heavy packs. The elevation gains and losses are challenging. The mountain range and the trail lie on a south-to-north axis, while the rivers that flow out of the Sierra run in an east-to-west direction. What this means is that mountain passes are laid out like gigantic hurdles. Ranging in elevation from 10,870 feet at Selden Pass to 13,117 feet at Forester Pass (the highest point on the Pacific Crest Trail), the passes are often covered with snow and ice well into July. A typical itinerary is to cross one pass a day, which means climbing 3,000 feet up, then 3,000 feet down, then walking along a valley where the trail crosses a series of rivers and streams that may early in the summer be swollen with snowmelt. Then you repeat the process, again, and again, and again.

The rewards are enormous: much of the JMT is above tree line—all of it is above 7,000 feet—and the twisty switchbacked climbs to each pass are scenic feasts. One of the most dramatic moments in any given day is reaching the crest of a pass and getting the first

glimpse of an entirely new and different world, with no sign of man, revealed in the new landscape ahead.

No sign of man, except, that is, for other hikers: July and August are peak season. Strict trailhead quotas are enforced along with camping regulations and bear-proofing protocols. Over the last 15 years, the problem of bear-human interactions over backpacking food in the Sierra has become so severe that strict bear-proofing regulations are in place. In certain areas, hikers are required to carry approved models of bear-proof canisters, which can be rented from the National Park Service.

As a result, there is something postmodern about today's High Sierra wilderness: this is not a wilderness where the hiker can have any illusion of being alone with nature, let alone being free from authority. Perhaps the saying that "we are loving our parks to death" is true. Certainly, a sense of wildness is compromised when it takes place under the careful watch of law-enforcement rangers checking permits in the middle of a wilderness. But without the regulations, the experience would be even more degraded from overuse, litter, and the habituation of wild animals to human food. Hikers who see such regulations as infringing on the experience of wilderness might better choose to hike elsewhere.

Usage levels notwithstanding, the fact remains that the John Muir Trail is something special: one of the nation's most scenic trails through one of the nation's largest wilderness complexes. This spectacular crown jewel of the American wilderness system is reserved for an exclusive crowd: not for those who can afford to pay for it, but for those who are willing to work for it. If you want to see Forester Pass, or Mather Pass, or any of the other high points where mountains stretch in both directions uninterrupted by any sign of habitation or construction, you must get there without any help from internal combustion engines, wheels, or electricity.

In his book *The Mountains of California*, Muir wrote, "Climb the mountains and get their good tidings. Nature's peace will flow into you as sunshine flows into trees. The winds will blow their own freshness into you, and the storms their energy, while cares will drop away from you like the leaves of Autumn."

His words resonate as strongly today as they did when they were published in 1894—and nowhere more so than on the trail that bears his name.

Painted Lady and Rae Lakes

KUNGSLEDEN

Sweden

When it comes to wilderness, orneriness grants a measure of protection. And the Arctic is nothing if not ornery. At first glance, Northern Sweden's Lapland has much in common with any other Arctic outpost. Inhabitants are few and far between, barely making an impression on the essential wildness of an expansive tundra landscape. Those who make their homes here are hardy and flexible, living in the state of flux that comes with constantly having to adapt to nature. The largely unspoiled Laponian region has been inscribed as a UNESCO World Heritage Site because of its geology, biology, and ecology, as well as its natural phenomena, and the culture of the native Sami people, whose semi-nomadic reindeer-herding lifestyle is centuries old.

What is different is that this northern wilderness can be accessed via a long-distance hiking trail. Trailheads are near regularly scheduled transportation routes, so hikers can get themselves here via a reasonable combination of planes, trains, and buses. With guidebooks, backcountry huts, and amenities such as occasional places to buy supplies, the Kungsleden—King of Trails—makes the cold heart of a far-north wilderness accessible to hikers with basic skills and equipment. In some sections of the trail (especially the popular far northern section), cabins offer beds and blankets. Bog bridges make walking easier while protecting fragile tundra from hiking boots. Boat services take hikers across lakes (or sometimes hikers row themselves, using boats provided for that purpose). And sturdy suspension bridges facilitate the crossing of rivers. Farther south, particularly in Sarek National Park, there are no roads, tracks, or bridges, making this terrain more suitable for experienced hikers.

Developed in the early 1900s, the approximately 270-mile-long trail lies between Abisko in the north and

View from Abiskojaure cabins, Kungsleden

Hemavan in the south. In the winter, a mostly contiguous route by the same name doubles as a ski trail. For winter trips, guided tours are recommended; the ski season begins in late February, when the stingy winter sun pokes above the horizon for at least a few hours a day, and lasts through April, when the snow begins to soften and the rivers begin to rise.

Meandering through four national parks and a nature reserve, the Kungsleden alternates between birch forests, open tundra, wide valleys, and rolling climbs, and passes enormous glaciers that feed roiling rivers. The highest point on the trail may be a mere 3,770 feet at Tjäktja Pass, but don't be lulled into complacency by the relatively modest elevations. At this latitude, that's plenty

high enough to remind the walker that here in the Far North, the Snow Queen never fully releases her grip.

The flora and fauna adjust accordingly. Trees—mostly birch and mountain ash—are stunted by winds that gallop unimpeded across the vast open spaces. As you gain elevation, dwarf willows and ferns give way to shrubs, bilberries, and reeds, along with delicate alpine flowers. The grasses, which shine an almost luminescent green in early summer, sustain large herds of reindeer. You might also see elk, lemmings (generally not doing anything nearly so interesting as following each other over suicidal cliffs), and a wide variety of birds. Wolverines and brown bears also inhabit the area, but are far less likely to be seen.

The original mountains here are old, with underlying rocks possibly related to those of the Scottish Highlands and the North American Appalachians. More recently, the mountains were covered by a two-mile-thick ice sheet that gouged out most of the landforms seen today, including U-shaped valleys, cliffs, waterfalls that tumble from hanging valleys, and lakes that collect water coming down from the glaciers. The scale of the land takes some getting used to: a mountain that seems just across the valley may in fact be a two-day walk away across a long stretch of flat tundra ringed by Arctic mountains.

This is a place where the light has that slanty high-latitude sharpness. Summer days last forever, with the solstice sun never fully sinking below the horizon. Colors are bright, almost fierce, especially in autumn when tundra grasses turn golden, lingonberries shimmer crimson, and the light angles and penetrates, seeming to intensify the already saturated blue of lakes and rivers. In winter, it is the night's turn to last forever, but nocturnal skies offer their own rewards: the shimmering auroral dance of the Northern Lights.

Through much of the route, the only settlements are very occasional communities of red-painted cabins, traditional tepees, and turf-covered huts used by the seminomadic Sami people, who travel through the area to hunt and herd their semidomesticated reindeer. This is the largest area in the world (and one of the last) with an ancestral way of life based on the seasonal movement of livestock.

Hikers find shelter in rustic huts located about eight to 15 miles apart from each other—about a day's walk—along most of the trail. Huts may be anathema to American wilderness sensibilities—as human constructions, they are seen as violating the very concept of wilderness. But here, they offer the only opportunities to resupply; hence, they make hiking possible. Don't expect the fancy catering common in refuges in the Alps. There's no refrigeration at the cabins, so the food is typical dried backpacking fare, and you cook it yourself. But you don't have to carry it, and neither do you have to carry a stove, gas, or cooking implements. If you plan to stay only in cabins, you won't need a tent or sleeping bag, either—blankets are provided. But you'll need a tent and sleeping bag for the southern half, where there are long sections with no cabins. Camping is permitted both near the cabins and in the wild. If you are camping, you can buy cooking fuel at some of the stations.

Hiking the entire Kungsleden takes a month or more, but the trail is easily divided into shorter segments, each about a week long. The most popular section begins at the far northern end in Abisko on Lake Torneträsk, and ends about 62 miles later at a roadhead near the Sami settlement of Nikkaluokta. In between are some of the trail's scenic highlights, including the majestic Tjäktjavagge Valley and Mount Kebnekaise, which at 6,926 feet is Sweden's highest peak. This section has enough cabins that you don't have to carry a tent, sleeping bag, cooking gear, or most of your food. From Nikkaluokta, it's less than an hour's drive to the regional center of Kiruna, which has an airport and a tourist bureau.

The Kungsleden is above the Arctic Circle, so the hiking season is short: cabins are open mid-June through September. Early summer is overrun with mosquitoes; midsummer is the most popular; late summer is the least crowded and least buggy, though with cold nights that start the vegetation turning gold.

Wilderness is, above all, about natural cycles: following them, experiencing them, falling into sync with them. Whether hiking or skiing, visitors to this unspoiled landscape soon respond to its rhythms, appreciating the short hours when sun shines in the winter, celebrating the endless days of summer. Perhaps the first lesson here is to live in harmony with the light. It is no surprise that most hikers walk the route southbound, so the Arctic sun can shine on their faces.

Reindeer family
along Kungsleden

TORRES DEL PAINE CIRCUIT

Chile

"Without doubt there are wild countries more favoured by Nature in many ways. But nowhere else are you so completely alone. Nowhere else is there an area of 100,000 square miles which you may gallop over, and where, whilst enjoying a healthy, bracing climate, you are safe from the persecutions of fevers, friends, savage tribes, obnoxious animals, telegrams, letters, and every other nuisance you are elsewhere liable to be exposed to."

So wrote Lady Florence Dixie in 1880, articulating feelings about wilderness that resonate today, some 140 years later. *Across Patagonia* is her account of what is thought to be the first foreign exploration of the area now known as Torres del Paine National Park. Traveling with a party consisting of her husband, her two brothers, another male friend, and several guides and camp staff, Lady Dixie rode on horseback into the wilds of Patagonia, sleeping in a tent for weeks on end.

In 1959, 80 years after her visit, the region she referred to as Cleopatra's Needles was protected as Parque Nacional de Turismo Lago Grey. In 1970, the name was changed to highlight the central massi f, Torres del Paine, whose 8,000- to 10,000-foot-tall granit e spires are the park's most famous vista. The park was designated a UNESCO World Biosphere Reserve in 1978.

Today's visitor has rather more company than Lady Dixie, whose small party met only a handful of nati ve Indians and one fugitive from the law during their explorations. Today about 140,000 people visit Torres del Paine National Park in a typical year. Most are here for the outdoor experience: kayaking, horseback riding, boating, fishing, bird watching, nature photography, and hiking. Day hikes can be made from *refugios* along the route or from lodges near park headquarters. The popular five-day W hike (so called because of its shape) takes in many of the park's highlights in about 31 miles.

Far fewer hikers tackle the *pièce de résistance*: a full circuit around the towers, pioneered in 1976 by a British mountaineer and two Torres del Paine rangers. The circuit is about 65 miles, give or take; the "give or take" is because of side trips to some of the trail's scenic highlights, which add distance but shouldn't be missed. As a result, most hikers plan a trek of eight to 10 days. Along with the shorter four- or five-day Mount Fitz Roy Trail in Argentina's Los Glaciares National Park, the Torres del Paine Circuit is considered one of Patagonia's most epic and scenic hikes.

The park is located a three-hour bus ride north of Punta Arenas, Chile, the world's southernmost city. It is a mountain wilderness where unrelenting forces—erosion, volcanism, and glaciations—have collided with severe weather—rain, snow, and unceasing wind—to carve a vertical landscape that is extreme even by mountain standards. Fantastical spires scrape the sky, much more than any building in Manhattan. Below the peaks, thundering glaciers calve into frigid glacial lakes.

The ecology here is equally extreme. As hikers climb through the park's elevations, they pass through a series of vegetation zones: Patagonian steppe, Pre-Andean shrubland, Magellanic subpolar forests, and then Andean desert. Native animals include wild guanacos (relatives of the llama), endangered Chilean huemuls (a species of deer—if you don't glimpse one here, you can find one on the Chilean national crest), and pumas, which hikers are unlikely to see. Lady Dixie, however, encountered several. Her lively and fascinating account is riddled with colonial attitudes toward the local people and a callousness toward the wildlife, which she seemed to enjoy mostly for the pleasure of hunting. "The guides all declared it to be the biggest puma they had ever seen," she wrote about one of the big cats unfortunate

Grey Glacier,
Torres del Paine Circuit

enough to cross her path. "The skin, which adorns the floor of the room where I am at present writing, measures exactly nine feet from the tip of the tail to the point of the nose."

The environment may be wild and challenging; it is also fragile and vulnerable, and not just in the usual ways (litter, soil compression at campsites, overcollection of wood for fires, pollution of water sources, and impact on animals). Surprisingly—considering the often rainy, foggy, and wet weather that soaks hikers to the bone—wildfire is part of the natural cycle of this ecosystem. During the rare dry spells, the vegetation is highly flammable. Fires set by careless hikers destroyed forests in 58 square miles of the park in 1985, 60 square miles in 2005, and 68 square miles in December and January of 2011–2012.

Partly as a result of these camping accidents, and also because of the popularity of the region, camping is allowed only near the refugios and in specified campsites. Wood fires are not permitted anywhere, and using

Fox near Hosteria,
Torres del Paine Circuit

OPPOSITE
Lake Pehoé and
Towers of Paine

a camping stove is also permitted only near the refugios. Refugios provide mattresses and sleeping bags, as well as food, beer and wine, and some equipment rentals. (For more luxurious hikes, guide services with pack transport are available.) Hikers can do the entire W trail using refugios, but on the Circuit, there are several stretches between huts that are longer than most trekkers can do in a day, so hikers should be prepared to camp. Tents that can handle strong winds are required. It's not unheard of for tent poles to snap during storms, and if you leave your tent unstaked for even a minute, it's likely to fly to Argentina.

Going counterclockwise, the trail's orange markers lead hikers along the Rio Paine to Lago Dickson, where views include the spiky peaks around Dickson and Los Perros Glaciers. A highlight—literally—is the climb to 4,429-foot John Gardner Pass. At the refuge at Grey Glacier, hikers can watch as humongous blocks of ice shear off the edge of the glacier and calve, noisily. Challenges on the trail include steep climbs, deep boot-sucking mud, winds that can stop you in your tracks, a subpolar mountain climate, and a few sections of trail where hikers must negotiate metal ladders, cables, or suspension bridges.

Prime hiking season is the southern summer, December through February, when temperatures top out in the low 60s and daylight lasts until about 10 p.m. It's also one of the drier times of year, although rain and fog are a predictable part of the equation. According to the widely used Köppen climate classification system, the park lies in the "temperate climate of cold rain without a dry season."

"I remember . . . many a discomfort," wrote Lady Dixie. ". . . the earthquake, the drenching rains, the scorching sun, the pitiless mosquitoes, and the terrible blasting winds. But from the pleasure with which I look back at my wild life in Patagonia, these unpleasant memories can detract but very little. Taking it all in all, it was a very happy time, and a time on whose like I would gladly look again."

OPPOSITE
Granite towers,
Torres del Paine Circuit

Flamingos on Paine Lake

Pyrenees High Route

France and Spain

It's traditional to dip your toes in the waters of the Atlantic Ocean at Hendaye Plage if you plan to walk over the top of the Pyrenees Mountains all the way to the Mediterranean Coast. And take a minute to find a pebble on the beach and put it in your pocket. That, too, is tradition.

Now face inland. To the left is France and to the right is Spain. Walk east, following red and white trail blazes out of town. You'll quickly find yourself climbing into the pastures of Basque Country. If you stay as close to the crest as trails allow, you'll be walking on what is known as the HRP (also the Pyrenees High Route, the Haute Randonnée Pyrénéene, the Haute Route Pyrénéene, or the Alta Ruta). Don't expect an easy hike: highly serrated, with unpredictable weather, the Pyrenees make an excellent international border. They've been thwarting travelers for hundreds of years.

There are actually three trails that traverse the Pyrenees from the Atlantic to the Mediterranean. A French route called the GR10 stays entirely in France; the GR11 stays in Spain. Closer to the crest, the HRP meanders about, now in Spain, then in France, for a short while in the tiny country of Andorra, and sometimes right on the border. The French GR10 is well marked and maintained, with readily available guidebooks and maps. The Spanish trail is less well marked, and guidebooks and maps are harder to find, especially if you're coming from outside of Spain. The HRP is clearly described in guidebooks; trail markings, however, are inconsistent and sometimes nonexistent. Each of the routes is around 560 miles long (guidebooks differ on the distance, and usually describe the journey in what they call stages, or daylong segments). If you are considering doing an entire traverse of the Pyrenees, figure 35 to 55 days, depending on speed and strength. For hikers interested in shorter treks, the GR10 and GR11 are easily accessible; both of

them dip into towns and villages, where hikers can buy supplies and sleep in inns or hostels.

The HRP stays closer to the crest. Hikers who don't care about the formalities of hiking an entire trail can piece together sections, cherry-picking from all three trails, staying in high mountain refuges for several days, and then descending into towns on the GR10 or the GR11 to resupply. However, hikers wanting to experience the heart of the HRP in the high mountains need to bring tents: there are places where refuges are too far apart for a day's walk. Maps, compasses, and a GPS are necessary to negotiate the many stretches where waymarks disappear. Some hikers bring ice axes for early summer snowfields. Some hikers don't—and wish they did. In cases of ice fields that linger late in the season and are too dangerous to cross, there are usually alternate routes available. Another option is waiting until later in the day when the snow softens enough to kick in steps.

The Pyrenees are often described as one of Western Europe's last wild areas outside of the Arctic wildernesses of Scandinavia. The HRP leads into the wildest, most remote parts of it. Even so, hiking in Europe has a distinctly different feel from an American wilderness experience. As is typical in Europe, refuge-to-refuge trekking, not wild camping, is the standard. When Europeans do camp, they tend to cluster around a refuge rather than seek out a lonely spot with no one in sight. In the popular national parks of the Pyrenees, it's hard to feel that you are in untrammeled wilderness when hiking on a trail with scores of others. And while the wine and three-course meal in a refuge at the end of the day are welcome, appreciated, and enjoyed, they are not a wilderness experience.

But while this is not wilderness in the American sense, it is a place where humans and the land have

Lakes from France/Spain frontier northeast of Núria, GR11

coexisted for centuries in a relationship that has left the sense of wildness very much intact. Indeed, this is one of the only regions in Western Europe that is wild enough to provide habitat for the endangered European brown bear. *Ursus arctos arctos* is the same species, although a distinctly different subspecies, as the brown bear (*Ursus arctos*) and the grizzly bear (*Ursus arctos horribilis*) found in North America. But unlike its big and fierce American cousins, the European brown bear has evolved into a shy animal that avoids contact with humans. After the last native brown bears in the Pyrenees were killed (probably by sheepherders) in the 1990s, a small group of bears from Slovenia was brought to the area. About 20 are thought to be currently surviving and breeding here, although a hiker would have to be very lucky to see one. Bringing back the bears has been fraught with tension that Americans familiar with the controversy over reintroducing wolves to the Northern Rockies will recognize. Bears eat lambs and sheep; herdsmen, though compensated by the government for livestock lost to bear predation, strongly oppose the reintroduction.

You'll see plenty of sheep as you begin the trek from the Atlantic climbing up into Basque Country, where unpronounceable place names are packed with consonants, with a special fondness for Xs and Zs. Herding is a traditional way of making a living here, and the grassy mountains offer summer pasturage. The summer climate is hot and humid, owing to moisture blowing in from the Atlantic. The trails here are not as well marked and maintained as they are in the heart of the mountains because they are not as popular with hikers.

In the center of the range, the mountain scenery is stunning on all three trails. The HRP spends more time above tree line and passes some of the region's best-known peaks and lakes, including the Vignemale (the highest peak in the French Pyrenees), Pic Aneto (the highest peak in the Spanish Pyrenees), Mont Perdu, Ordesa Canyon, Parc National des Pyrénées (in France), and Parque Nacional de Aiguas Tortas y Lago de San Mauricio (in Spain).

The climate in the Pyrenees is notoriously variable, but as you continue to walk, a few patterns emerge: the French side is rainier and cloudier than the Spanish side. The Atlantic side is wetter and more humid than the Mediterranean side, where the land turns frankly harsh, with sandy soils covered with typical dryland Mediterranean scrub.

This change in vegetation is your first notice that the walk is drawing to an end. Confirmation comes with the thirst of sun-baked climbs, followed by the relentless descent to the sea. Now try to remember where you put that pebble you picked up on the beach in Hendaye. When you reach the rocky beach on the Mediterranean Coast at Banyuls sur Mer, lay it in the water. Having carried a rock clear across the Pyrenees, it's time to lay down your burden.

OVERLAND TRACK

Australia

Wallabies hop through the tall grass. A currawong grasps a backpack zipper in his beak and starts to undo it. A snake slithers by: there's a 100 percent chance it's venomous. Wildlife sightings take on a whole new meaning for hikers on the Overland Track, a 40-mile bush walk through Cradle Mountain–Lake Saint Clair National Park in the Tasmanian Wilderness World Heritage Area. The advice offered to hikers sets the stage: bring a salt solution to repel leeches. Bring a pack cover to protect packs from carrawongs and ravens that have learned to open zippers, clips, and Velcro. And about those snakes: all species on the island are venomous, though usually not aggressive.

Other animals might include common campground visitors like opossums and mice and a host of critters you won't recognize from home: wombats, pademelons (small forest-dwelling marsupials), eastern crolls (they combine the head of a squirrel, the spots of a newborn fawn, and the tail of a cat), platypuses, echidnas, and, just maybe, Tasmanian devils.

The island has long caught the attention of visitors: Charles Darwin, who visited in 1836, praised it for its climate; Anthony Trollope called it the prettiest of all colonies. And Mark Twain wrote, "How beautiful is the whole region, for form, and grouping, and opulence, and freshness of foliage, and variety of colour, and grace and shapeliness of the hills, the capes, the promontories; and then, the splendour of the sunlight, the dim rich distances, the charm of the water-glimpses!"

Much of the island remains in the same wild state: about 40 percent of Tasmania is preserved as wilderness, including the entire Overland Track. The lush vegetation and rich foliage that caught the eye of early visitors delight hikers today as they make their way through temperate rain forest, eucalyptus forest, alpine moorlands,

and button grass plains (that means swamp). Rain forest evergreens like myrtle beech, celery-top pine, and sassafras keep the lower slopes green throughout the winter, although the fagus—a small beech that is Tasmania's only deciduous tree—turns golden in April and early May (autumn in this part of the world). Higher up, the striking pandani palms—grass trees that can resemble the weird Afro-Alpine groundsels of East Africa's volcanoes—stand as sentinels in the mountains. Surrounding them are spiny thickets of pink-flowering *richea scoparia* (famed for its impenetrability) and carpets of alpine herbs, shrubs, mosses, and cushion plants.

The track is mostly well defined and easy to follow, but trail conditions can vary, especially after sustained periods of heavy rain. An unusual feature here are the boardwalks, called duckboard, some of which are hundreds of feet long. Embedded over boggy stretches of trail likely to flood, they protect the hikers' feet from the mud—and fragile vegetation from tromping boots. In good weather, the trail presents no unusual challenges except for the long steady climbs that take hikers from the rain forest zone to the alpine zone, and a few steep sections where walking sticks will aid with balance. In rainy weather, the mud can be daunting, and in freezing temperatures, ice forms, turning duckboards into something more like a skating rink than a hiking trail.

About 8,000 walkers brave the elements and complete the trek each year. The trail can be hiked any time of year, but to preserve the feeling of wildness, a quota system limits traffic to 60 hikers a day during the high season (October 1 through May 31). Permits should be booked in advance with Tasmania's Parks and Wildlife Service. Walkers typically complete the trek in about six days, usually hiking from north to south (the mandatory direction of travel during the high season).

Overland Track approaching
Lake Saint Clair

FOLLOWING SPREAD
Wallaby along
Overland Track

In addition to the main trail, more than 19 miles of side trails lead to nearby highlights, including Cradle Mountain, Mount Pelion, a group of tarns called The Labyrinth, and the fluted dolorite columns of Mount Ossa, which at 5,305 feet is Tasmania's highest peak. If that's not long enough, it is possible to continue the hike along Lake Saint Clair for another 11 miles. The track has huts spaced a few miles apart, but there is no reservation system, so hikers must bring a tent and sleeping bag in case the huts are full. The huts provide bunks, but no food or stoves. Open fires are not permitted.

It is interesting that both Trollope and Darwin praised the weather: perhaps they weren't in this part of the island, or maybe they were lucky enough to miss the region's extremes. In summer, temperatures can top 95°F or plummet so low that sleet and snow coat the duckboards. Not to mention the wind: Tasmania's location on a latitude of 40 degrees south puts it directly in the path of the "Roaring Forties," which can flatten a tent and force a hiker to turn around. Hikers are reminded that Cradle Mountain is reputed to have only 32 clear days a year, so clothing bags should include rain gear and enough layers for cold, wet, miserable weather. On the plus side, when the sun shines, the scenery is simply unforgettable: mountains carved by glaciers into cirques and peaks, lakes and tarns, gorges and waterfalls.

Irish journalist John Mitchel was apparently one of the lucky ones. He visited Tasmania in 1850 and wrote, "It is a soft blue day; soft airs, laden with all the fragrances of those antarctic woods, weave an atmosphere of ambrosia around me. As we coast along over the placid waters, passing promontory after promontory, wooded to the water's edge, and 'glassing their ancient glories in the flood' both sea and land seem to bask and rejoice in the sunshine."

Then again, this is a landscape whose ecology and geography were shaped by wild weather. It is somehow fitting to experience its various temperamental moods, which are so often followed by the sort of pristine clear days enjoyed by some of the poets, explorers, and writers who visited here so long ago.

MORE WILDERNESS WALKS

Long Range Traverse, Canada

They call it "the Rock" and it is wilderness almost by definition: perched in the frigid North Atlantic, Newfoundland was abandoned when the Vikings visited in the 11th century, and even today, it has one of the lowest human population densities in the world. So it's no surprise that the 20-mile Long Range Traverse in Gros Morne National Park is a test of wilderness hiking skills. There are no trail markers but plenty of caribou, elk, and bear paths, which might lead you astray as you make your way through coastal fjords, granite cliffs, spruce groves, heather fields, peat bogs, and krummholz (wind-twisted tundra bushes; literally "crooked trees"). Indeed,

at a mandatory orientation, hikers are quizzed on their navigation skills before being allowed to proceed on the journey, and then given a locator device for good measure. The hike begins with a deceptively easy two-mile trail to the ferry, followed by an hour-long boat ride and a long steady climb into the interior. After that, all bets are off as you scramble and try to find your way through a navigational maze of forests, mountains, and ponds. The hike takes about five days (the low mileage is a result of the navigational and terrain challenges, plus the need to hold a day or two for bad weather). On the last day, take a side trail to 2,644-foot Gros Morne Mountain, and before you get complacent about the low altitude, consider the latitude: this is an arctic-alpine zone, high above tree line, buffeted by constant winds. For obvious reasons, this is a summer hike. Reservations and permits are required.

Lost Coast Trail, United States

This 25-mile trail in California is one of only a handful of wilderness coastal hiking experiences in the contiguous United States. This mostly flat walk hugs the exact place where land meets sea at the base of the rocks where the King Range plunges into the Pacific. Initially slated to be developed as part of the Pacific Coast Highway, the wilderness was saved when engineers got a firsthand look at the cliffs and the ocean and skedaddled inland to build the road in a more sane location. It's not even fully passable for hikers: ocean waves can be dangerously high and sometimes spray onto the trail; spring snowmelt can swell streams that run down from the mountains; and some parts of the route are passable only at low tide (carry tide tables and bring your patience). Indeed, taking your time is good advice for the whole trail: figure at least three days to enjoy the sea lions, sea otters, tidal pools, and wildflowers. This hike through Bureau of Land Management lands can be crowded in summer: spring and fall offer more chances for solitude.

Long Range Traverse,
Canada

OPPOSITE
Lost Coast Trail,
California, United States

Larapinta Trail, Australia

Aussies are more likely to use the word "bush" than the word "wilderness," but that is mere semantics on the Larapinta Trail, a 139-mile trek through the outback of the Northern Territory. Views along this desert mountain path seem to stretch to infinity, with little or no sign of people, except on the trail itself, where excellent waymarks, trailheads, water tanks, and campsites make the hiker's job a little easier. The trail is easily divided into one- to two-day segments; the entire trail can be completed in 15 to 20 days, preferably in the cooler months between May and August. The route takes walkers through MacDonnell National Park from the old Alice Springs Telegraph Station to Mount Sonder, offering expansive views of vast flood plains, razorback ridges, and, at night, impossibly starry skies. Sacred to the indigenous Arrernte people, the mountain ranges are believed to be gigantic caterpillars or "Yeperenye," who were the most important of the creative ancestors of Alice Springs; the water hole at Glen Helen is home to a rainbow serpent. Challenges include desert heat, lack of water, flash floods, the possibility of dingoes trying to pillage your pack for food, and a sneak attack by the spinifex—a plant with needle-sharp spikes that can poke holes in an air mattress.

Pacific Northwest Trail, United States

This mighty 1,200-mile path takes in the entire wilderness landscape of the great Northwest from Montana to Washington, starting in Glacier National Park and hugging the Canadian border through the Northern Rockies and the North Cascades, and then crossing the Olympic Peninsula. Designated a national scenic trail in 2011, the Pacific Northwest Trail transects the predominantly north-south mountain ranges, making for dramatic elevation changes. One of the highlights is the old-growth forests, with giant western hemlocks, Douglas firs, and western red cedars, some of which can be 1,000 years old. Don't expect much company on the trails here. A thru-hike takes about three months; most of the trail is only accessible in summer.

Highline Trail, United States

The backbone of the Wind River Mountains is the Continental Divide. This 80-mile trek loosely parallels the Divide from Green River Lakes Trailhead to Big

Larapinta Trail, Australia

FOLLOWING SPREAD
Pacific Northwest Trail,
Washington, United States

GREAT HIKING TRAILS OF THE WORLD

Sandy Lodge in Wyoming. A network of hiking trails and off-trail routes makes it possible to customize your hike to follow the Continental Divide Trail, to venture even closer to the physical Divide, or to loop back via the Fremont Trail. Whichever route you choose, this is one of the most beautiful mountain hikes in the world, almost always above 10,000 feet. Late August and early September are ideal: the mosquitoes and snow are long gone, the willows and upland grasses start turning a burnished gold, and the quaking aspen shine a bright sun-filled yellow.

High Sierra Trail, United States

A less-crowded alternative to the John Muir Trail, the High Sierra Trail in California begins in Giant Forest in Sequoia National Park, and crosses the Sierra range from west to east, ending 49 miles later at Wallace Creek and the junction with the John Muir Trail. However, that's not the end of the hiking: you still have to make your way out, either by retracing your steps, or by continuing on the John Muir Trail 12.6 miles to the Mount Whitney summit and another 11 miles down the other

Highline Trail,
Montana, United States

side to the Whitney Portal Trailhead. A challenging climb on the second day leads over the Great Western Divide at Kaweah Pass, but it comes with eye-popping views of Hamilton Lake and a sea of mountains on either side. The first day of this hike is popular; after that, you are likely to be on your own.

Mount Fitz Roy Trail, Argentina

Before being named for the captain of the HMS *Beagle*, Monte Fitz Roy was known as the Cerro Chaltén—"Smoking Mountain"—not for any volcanic fumes, but for the clouds that seemed to emanate from its summit. That should tell you something about the weather. Argentina's answer to the Torres del Paine, 11,171-foot Monte Fitz Roy is the centerpiece of Los Glaciares National Park, with triangular spires whose famous profiles are instantly recognizable to mountaineers worldwide. The park is a UNESCO World Heritage Site, inscribed for its wild character and enormous glaciers and ice fields. Several route variations allow hikes of between two and five days: a classic 12-mile trek can be done in two days, although with the region's famously terrible weather, it's best to have a couple of extra days in your schedule so you don't miss the spectacle of sunrise over the granite spires. A full circuit of the mountain is about 36 miles, requires some glacier walking, and takes approximately four to five days depending on how many forays you take to viewpoints. Prime trekking season is from November to April; March and April have fewer people and marginally better weather.

High Sierra Trail,
California, United States

FOLLOWING SPREAD
Mount Fitz Roy Trail, Argentina

CHAPTER 5

EXPLORING DIVERSITY

When early tourists to the Grand Canyon expressed a desire to hike to the bottom, they were met with incredulity: Why on earth didn't they do what everyone else did—ride a mule? On the other side of the country, in subtropical Florida, the impetus to create a statewide hiking resource—what is now the Florida Trail—arose from an utter lack of hiking trails in the state. Well into the 1960s, if you lived in Florida and wanted to backpack, you needed to head north somewhere, to Georgia or North Carolina perhaps. • But just as ancient humans walked through, and to, the world's most extreme environments—jungles and tundra and deserts—modern backpackers do the same. Mountain landscapes may have the pride of place on hikers' bucket lists, but they are far from the only places to hike. The dramas of wilderness—the dance of predator and prey, the cycles of weather events, the seasonal changes of flowers and foliage—take place

on beaches, along coastal cliffs, in deserts, on moors, in tundra, in swamps, and in old-growth forests. Hiking gives us a way to interact with these landscapes. The only limits are our own ruggedness and our ability to adapt to the challenges some of these environments present.

Different rules apply: desert rules are different from mountain rules are different from rain forest rules are different from tundra rules. That means a different skill set, different gear choices, and most of all, a different mind-set. Some examples:

In America's Southwest, or in Australia's interior, the combination of water shortages and high temperatures in the summer months can be life-threatening, with air temperatures above 100°F and ground temperatures that can burn through the soles of a pair of trekking shoes. Hikers learn which seasons to avoid, and even in cooler temperatures, they learn to hike with water on the brain, always monitoring which springs are running, which ones are dry, and how long it will take to navigate to the next certain source.

In the old-growth forests of the Pacific Northwest, hikers walk through a mythically proportioned landscape—one whose magic is created in no small part by rain and clouds and a wet season that lives up to its name. But even in drier times of year, this is a place that demands a workable system for living in the rain: during the periodic storms, you'll need to know how to keep gear dry while pitching and striking a tent, how to cook and eat, and how to stay dry while walking.

In the tundra of the Far North—in places like Iceland or Lapland—the margin of error decreases as the latitude increases. Fog and snow may obscure the trail at any time of year, so navigation skills are important. As important is the ability to regulate body temperature and gear so you stay warm while alternating between hiking and stopping to navigate.

Depending on the destination and season, specialized equipment might be required: gum boots for the jungle, snowshoes for the tundra, lightweight trekking shoes for the desert, stiff-soled boots for cramponing in icy mountains. Your choice of a tarp or tent system will depend on what you need protection from: rain, snow, bugs, cold, or wind. Even food planning is entirely different: the cheeses and chocolates that work so well in Iceland melt into a gooey mess in Arizona; the tinned

foods that don't spoil in Florida freeze in Patagonia. And don't pack crackers for snacking if you're planning to hike through a rain forest. They are likely to melt on the way from the ziplock bag to your mouth!

The challenges can sometimes be surprising. Hikers accustomed to the rhythms of mountain hiking usually base their expectations for difficulty, pace, and mileage on the elevation. How high is the mountain? How steep is the grade? How much elevation will they gain and lose in a day? Trails in flatter terrain like shorelines or forests don't have the same bumpy profile, so hikers often underestimate the potential difficulties, not realizing, for instance, that the easy-looking beach walk is actually a long slog through soft sand that can be every bit as challenging as climbing a thousand feet. The same is true with trudging through sucking mud. And a trail that climbs and descends a piddly 250 feet—but does so 20 times in a day—has still gained (and lost) an exhausting 5,000 feet of elevation. It's worth remembering that it doesn't take

PREVIOUS SPREAD
Laugavegurinn Trail, Iceland

OPPOSITE
Ice Age Trail,
Wisconsin, United States

Arizona Trail,
Arizona, United States

a mountain to challenge a hiker: Vancouver Island's West Coast Trail makes it on many a hiker's "most difficult" list despite a high point of only 690 feet above sea level.

It's not all hard work. At the right time of year, with the right gear (and sometimes, with a bit of luck), many of these environments offer pleasant, even easy conditions. In spring, winter, or fall, with maps that accurately show reliable water sources, desert hiking offers a downright comfortable experience, with little threat of rain, warm daytime temperatures, cool dry evenings, and few bugs. Get lucky with your timing and the weather in a temperate rain forest, and you might walk through the giant groves in a constant state of wonder as sunlight streams through the canopy. Even when the weather gods do not cooperate, hikers with the right gear and skills can be overwhelmed by the power of the landscape and the forces that continue to shape it.

The trails that follow were chosen neither for their ease nor for their difficulty, but for their variety—for how they represent some of the other prime ecosystems for hikers, whether coastlines, lakeshores, canyons, deserts, tundra, or swamps. Some of them require advanced skills; others, especially some of the temperate coastline walks, are gentle strolls through easy terrain. All of these landscapes have their own aficionados, in love with the views, the scope of the land, the varied geology and geographies, and the fascinating adaptations of the native plants and animals. There is a special beauty in these extremes: in the expanse of a desert landscape, the solitude of a canyon, the vastness of a trackless beach, or the majesty of old-growth forests that were seedlings before the first Vikings set foot on North American shores.

And in each of these distinct ecosystems, there are the countless moments of micro-magic—reflections on water, patterns in the sand, sunlight through the trees, rainbows in a raindrop—that elevate our hiking experience from something merely recreational to something transcendent.

Great Ocean Walk, Australia

THE MILFORD TRACK

New Zealand

Arthur River, South Island

OPPOSITE
Wetland area
along Milford Track

They will tell you it will rain. They might even say, in the friendliest way possible, that they hope it does. A lot. And you will wonder, what kind of person wishes rain on a backpacker? Whether they wish it or not, whether you like it or not, it probably will rain. The southwest part of the South Island of New Zealand is said to be one of the wettest places on earth.

So it is interesting that the 33-mile Milford Track, which goes through this predictably wet place, is known far and wide as the "finest walk in the world." The epithet dates to 1908, when Kiwi poet Blanche Baughan turned in an essay to the *London Spectator*. The editor had an eye for headlines. He changed the title she'd written—"A Notable Walk"—to something he thought was catchier: "The Finest Walk in the World." The claim has stuck for more than a century.

The basic profile of the Milford Track is up and down, from lake to sea with a high mountain pass in the middle. On either side are two enormous U-shaped glacial valleys with steep rock walls. The highest waterfall in New Zealand, 1,900-foot Sutherland Falls, is accessible via a short side trail.

There are two ways to "tramp" (as it's called in New Zealand) this popular trail through the South Island Fiordlands. On a guided trip, trampers stay in plush huts where food is prepared for them, and there is no need to carry sleeping bags. On independent treks, hikers carry their own gear and food, make their own meals, and sleep in a communal hostel. They also find their own way, though on this well-marked and well-maintained track, navigation is hardly a challenge, even when the fog swirls in, which it does. Only 90 permits are available each day, 50 for guided hikers and 40 for independent trekkers. The cost differential is enormous, and the trek is both short enough and easy enough that trampers don't need all that much help. As a result, independent permits sell out months in advance.

The base for this hike is Te Anau, a small Fiordland town where the Milford Track and the adjacent (and also spectacular) Kepler Track are two of the main businesses. At the ranger station, hikers pick up the coveted permits, along with a dose of Kiwi attitude about the rain. The rangers will tell you that no matter what rain you've experienced, you haven't experienced what it can do here, and pictures of trails flooded waist deep support the contention. Enormous, thick pack-liner bags are available for purchase to keep your gear dry.

The trek begins with a boat ride across Lake Te Anau, the second-largest freshwater lake in New Zealand. Even in summer, the surrounding peaks will be capped by snow. The independent Milford Track is a three-night, four-day hike, pretty much divided by following the Clinton River up the valley, climbing to Mackinnon Pass, and then going down the Arthur Valley on the other side to end at Sandfly Point on Milford Sound. Note the name "Sandfly Point." Sandflies are New Zealand's answer to midges; a Māori legend says that the gods, realizing they had created an earthly paradise, wanted to keep the region to themselves so they added sandflies to keep people away.

Independent and guided trampers depart at different times on different boats and follow different schedules, so they never meet. For independent trekkers, the first day is a short flat walk to Clinton Hut, nestled in a forest with cliffs looming overhead. Nice enough, but it doesn't quite have the "finest walk in the world" vibe.

But when it rains . . .

Cats, dogs, buckets, sheets, lashing, pouring: a foot or more can fall in a single day. Most of the time, treks go on despite the weather. After all, 90 more people are just a day behind, permits in hand, waiting for their place in the bunkhouses. However, in vicious storms the water on the trails through the valleys can rise several feet, delaying hikers for several hours or (rarely) for a day or more. Helicopter evacuations are rare, but occasionally necessary.

After a day's heavy rain, you'll understand why people say this is a trail that is beautiful in sunshine, but best seen in rain. The massive walls of rock that line the valley turn into waterfalls, hundreds of them, each hundreds of feet in height. When the wind is fierce, it rips the water right out of the air and flings it across the valley.

Nature has many faces: gentle and healing, whimsical, awe inspiring. Think snowflakes, moonlit lakes, aardvarks, and Mount Everest. On the Milford Track, nature can be an easy companion as you stroll up the scenic mountain pass, or it can be nature in the guise of power: God having a temper tantrum; rain falling in sheets; waterfalls, for crying out loud, blowing sideways.

Weather like that puts you in your own encapsulated space. You can't talk to your hiking partner because they can't hear you, what with nylon hoods crackling about and pelting torrents and howling wind. You can't stop walking or you'll get cold. Taking pictures is out of the question without a full-on underwater camera. All you can really do is feel the enormous power of the land, and your own power walking through it: the wind, the rain, and your progress, step by step, moving in regular motion, your breath, your heart.

The view from Mackinnon Pass is certainly up there in the "finest walk in the world" category, If, that is, you get a chance to see its snow-covered peaks and the hovering clouds that create their patchwork of light and shadow. On the other side of the pass is Sutherland

OPPOSITE
Mackinnon Pass,
Milford Track

Roaring Burn Waterfall,
Milford Track

Falls, although in heavy rain, the combination of the falls themselves and the added water from the sky—pounding down, bouncing up, flying sideways—makes it impossible to get close without getting as thoroughly drenched as if you had simply dived into the river. And, of course, all that water needs somewhere to go, which is why you saw those pictures back at the ranger station—the ones of hikers trekking through water up to their thighs.

So, to sum up the experience: rain, cliffs, rain, waterfalls, rain, a spectacular mountain pass, rain. Then a high, fierce, skin-soaking waterfall. More rain, more cliffs, more rain, more waterfalls. Perhaps a kea bird. Perhaps some flooded trail. And finally, cliff-lined Milford Sound. Also, good company in the huts, knowledgeable rangers, well-marked trail, and, if you're lucky, a propitious break in the weather to let you see Mackinnon Pass, the trail's scenic highlight.

What makes a trail the "finest walk in the world"? Certainly scenery is part of the picture, but every mountain range has scenery. Unspoiled nature is part of it, but there again, there's a lot of competition. The Dr. Seuss forests on Mount Kenya? The old-growth red cedars of the North Cascades? The enormous treeless tundra of Iceland? Is one finer than the other? What is this obsession we have with "best"? Is there even such a thing as "better than" when it comes to nature and mountains and forests? And how would Blanche Baughan and her editor have known, anyway, when they agreed to call the Milford Track the finest walk in the world? It's not like they had walked all over the planet.

Still there is no denying that the Milford Track packs a mass of superlatives into its 33 miles: New Zealand's second-largest lake, its highest waterfall, certainly one of its most scenic passes. But there is also the quality of the experience. Waist-high water flooding the trail and waterfalls blowing sideways may not be everyone's cup of tea, but the sheer power of the experience eclipses so many others. It's the kind of adventure that sticks with you, years later, when you are spinning stories and mining memories.

Mackay Falls, Milford Track

TONTO TRAIL

United States

It is almost impossible to imagine what it would be like to come upon this vast hole into the guts of the earth with no foreknowledge of it. The first European known to have viewed Arizona's Grand Canyon was García López de Cárdenas, from Spain, who arrived in 1540. Cárdenas would have approached the Grand Canyon from the south through a flattish landscape of pinyon forest. There is no warning of what lies ahead. One minute, you are navigating through the pinyons and junipers, then the forest ends, the earth opens, and you peer a full mile into a canyon that could swallow all of Manhattan and leave room for several more of the world's biggest cities.

Little information about the Cárdenas expedition has trickled down to us through time, but the explorer seems to have had trouble understanding the size and scope of what he was seeing. Looking into the maw that opened a mile beneath his feet, Cárdenas thought the river was a trickle, but when he sent men down to try to obtain water, they made it only a third of the way before turning back. It would be more than 200 years before the next serious European exploration of the area.

The scale of the Grand Canyon still befuddles, even though hikers know what lies ahead from pictures. It is landscape that does not fit easily into the human brain. Hiking for fun is a relatively new activity in Grand Canyon National Park. Since the late 1880s, the accepted way to travel into the canyon was to hire a wrangler and ride a mule. Today, a network of hiking trails leads into and along the canyon. But, as Cárdenas's men learned firsthand, Grand Canyon hiking is not easy: the National Park Service strongly recommends that first-time visitors and hikers with little or no desert experience stick to the main corridor trails—the South Kaibab Trail and the Bright Angel Trail on the South Rim, and the North Kaibab Trail on the North Rim—which are wider, well

Granite Gorge and the
Colorado River, Tonto Trail

maintained, and patrolled. (These trails are also used by the mules, which still carry overnight visitors and their gear to the bottom and back.) Even so, every year hikers ignore the warnings or overestimate their strength; there is no shortage of work for the search-and-rescue teams and the on-site nursing staff.

So first things first: the 95-mile Tonto Trail is a challenging backcountry trail that requires navigation skills, the ability to make efficient use of scarce water sources, and a certain degree of comfort on scrabbly, rocky trails. Most hikers don't tackle the entire 95 miles. The Tonto Trail intersects all of the South Rim cross-canyon trails, so hikers can create in-and-out hikes of varying lengths. Those who venture into this less-visited part of the canyon, whether for a weekend or a week, will have an experience completely unlike that of the streams of hikers who congregate on the major trails.

The Tonto Trail generally parallels the south bank of the Colorado River, from its eastern end at the junction with the Red Canyon Trail to the western end at Garnet Canyon. In between, it mostly stays on the Tonto Platform, which is the easily identifiable wide green layer you see when looking down from the rim. This is the layer that separates the Grand Canyon's inner gorge from its upper canyon. By staying on this level, the trail mostly avoids long, steep climbs (once you are in and out of the canyon, that is). Instead, it contours in and out of a seemingly unending series of side canyons. Distance is relative: the in-and-outs can add many miles to what might appear to be a short distance as the crow flies.

The Tonto Trail is nothing like the mule-worthy corridor trails: its narrow treadway is sometimes hard to see and easy to lose, or it can be confused with animal paths. Because the Tonto Trail is less commonly used than the major corridor trails, permits for overnight backpacking are easier to get, and campsites are less crowded. Indeed, it is sometimes possible to spend an entire winter week and see hardly any hikers, except on the section that connects the South Kaibab and Bright Angel Trails.

The hike can be extended at either end. At the western end, it is possible to hike a little farther to Elves Chasm on trail that is steep, unstable, and sometimes difficult to navigate. But having made it this far, most hikers find the side trip to the waterfall-fed pool well worth the work. On the eastern end, the Tonto Trail turns into the riverside Escalante Route and Beamer Trail. Both are accessed by the Tanner Trail, which leaves the South Rim at Lipan Point and descends through 4,600 feet of sometimes loose rock to the junction of the Colorado and Little Colorado Rivers.

The most popular (and best-maintained) section of the Tonto Trail is the four miles between the South Kaibab and Bright Angel Trails, which makes it possible to hike a 13-mile horseshoe. (Shuttle buses can get you from one trailhead to another.) However, this is a stiff 13-mile hike involving a steep downhill walk, a flattish crossing on the Tonto Trail, and then a 3,000-foot straight-up climb from Indian Garden to the South Rim. Hikers who don't already have considerable experience with this kind of mileage and elevation should break the hike up into a two-day backpack trip: the first day would include the four-and-a-half-mile downhill section on the Kaibab Trail and the four-mile flat hike on the Tonto Trail; the overnight would be spent at Indian Garden (permits are required); and the four-and-a-half-mile climb up the Bright Angel Trail would take place on the second day.

Desert rules apply here, and first and foremost, that means water: thinking about it, drinking it, planning for it, rationing it, treating it, and, above all, respecting it. The main threat is dehydration: hikers unacclimated to desert heat and aridity may need much more water than they do when hiking similar distances and elevations in gentler climates. Similarly, heat exhaustion is a threat in the warmer months, when canyon temperatures can soar above 100°F. Some water sources are seasonal, which means they don't run all year. All wild water in the canyon should be treated, with the exception of the water at Indian Garden, which is potable. In addition to dehydration and heat exhaustion, potential hazards include flash flooding, loose footing, rockfall, rattlesnakes, and, in winter, ice—sometimes at inconvenient spots where a fall would be deadly.

Hiking the entire Tonto Trail is not for everyone. Certainly, gaining experience on other Grand Canyon trails first is necessary, as is having some familiarity with desert environments. But for hardy hikers with good skills, the Tonto Trail is a magical way to leave the crowds completely behind and experience the massive silences, the grand scope, and the endlessly changing vistas and colors of one of the natural wonders of the world.

Prickly pear cactus along Tonto Trail

West Coast Trail

Canada

It was never intended to be a hiking trail. When the first paths were cut on the southwest coast of British Columbia's Vancouver Island, the thought of bashing through this obstruction-filled forest for recreation would have been laughable, if not insane.

First Nations people had been living here, but they'd had 4,000 years to figure out how to navigate the thick forests and roiling seas. When the first Europeans arrived in the late 19th century to install a telegraph line, they found themselves surrounded by land that was difficult to move through and a section of ocean where storms sank so many ships that it became known as the Graveyard of the Pacific. Shipwreck victims who reached land had to fight their way through a fecund temperate rain forest where undergrowth, mud, cliffs, and rocks blocked the way. In 1906, after 133 people aboard the SS *Valencia* were drowned, the Dominion Lifesaving Trail was built so that rescuers could have easier access to the coast, and survivors of shipwrecks who by some miracle made it to shore would have a prayer of finding their way out.

The trail fell into disuse as railroads reached the region, and lay forgotten until 1976, when it was resurrected as part of the hiking boom of the 1970s. Today, the West Coast Trail, managed by Pacific Rim National Park, is known as one of the toughest hiking trails in the world. Also one of the best.

When long-distance hikers with high-mountain experience first learn about the West Coast Trail, they can't reconcile its modest statistics with its outsized reputation. The West Coast Trail never climbs a single mountain, and the high point of the entire route is a measly 690 feet. Yet although it is a mere 48 miles long, it can take a week—or more—to hike it. For hikers used to friendlier trails, the numbers don't add up.

Until you look at the obstacles, which do. This is a land where old-growth spruce, hemlock, and western red cedars hold up the sky. When ancient trees topple, it can be a major climbing project just to get from one side to the other. In the forests that grow just behind the tide line, fallen trees lie atop one another like a giant's carelessly discarded pile of pick-up sticks. Rotting trunks are covered with mosses and epiphytes, finally decomposing into a rich nursery in which new trees can grow.

Rocks and cliffs alternate with deadfall, spongy moss-covered ground sinks underfoot, and roots the size of anacondas lie in the way. Not to mention puddles

View of Strait of
Juan de Fuca and the
Olympic Peninsula

OPPOSITE
Boardwalk through forest
along inland section of
West Coast Trail

of mud that can swallow an incautious hiker up to the thigh. Boardwalks lead over some of the worst obstacles, but in rain, the wood can be slick. Sturdy wooden ladders lead up, over, and around the cliffs that block the way, but make for slow going. On the beach, hikers alternate between picking their way through boulders, clambering over more fallen trees, and struggling through soft sand.

And then there is the matter of water, which is constantly eroding, carving, and flooding the landscape. Some streams and rivers are forded by means of rock hopping or crossing on fallen logs. Some are crossed via suspension bridges that swing underfoot with each step. And a few require climbing into a precarious-looking metal cage and riding it on a steel cable halfway across—then ratcheting yourself up the other side by pulling hand-over-hand while dangling a hundred or more feet above the rushing water.

Obstacles, rain, falls, hypothermia—in the average hiking season, one person is rescued from the trail every other day. The trail's ornery reputation doesn't dissuade hikers. Indeed, the West Coast Trail is one of Canada's best-known trails, and has become so popular that a quota system is in place; the 8,000 permits that are available starting every March 16 are quickly snapped up. A few are held for walk-in hikers, but there's no guarantee: hikers who just show up may have to wait a few days before a permit becomes available.

Challenge is one of the trail's attractions. The other is its unique environment: the combination of a wild North Pacific beach with forests whose trees may be 1,000 years old or more. On the beaches, hikers will find ocean-framed cliffs, headlands, whales, shipwrecks, puffins, eagles, tidal flats and tidal pools, caves, crabs, orange and purple-brown starfish, coves, rock arches, sea stacks, and sea lions. Inland in the forest are old-growth trees, waterfalls, river otters, bears, cougars, and the wild, primeval sound of wolves howling into the infinity of night. And on both the shore and in the forest: pristine wilderness, ocean sunsets, fog, rain, and the adrenaline-producing sense of exhilaration that comes from living among all of this for a week.

In some ways, this trail is all about attitude. With the possible exception of being able to read a tide table and knowing enough not to pitch your tent where high tide will drown you in the middle of the night, hikers need no special skills to hike the West Coast Trail. For the most part, the obstacles found here—boulders, scrambles, mud puddles, ladders, cable crossings, and fallen trees—are found on many other trails, in many other environments.

This trail simply has more of them per mile. Climbing a ladder is followed by slogging through mud is followed by scrambling over a fallen tree is followed by pulling yourself across a river on a cable car. It's slow going. But once hikers adjust their expectations to realize that a seven-mile day is making fine time, half the battle is won, and the fun can begin.

LAUGAVEGURINN TRAIL

Iceland

Elves live here. Trouble when building a house? Maybe the elves don't like its location. Accidents on a highway? Perhaps it goes through an elf community. Lost in the backcountry? Maybe an elf will show up to guide you out. There are even elf whisperers, said to be able to communicate between the human world and the elfish one.

According to a study by the University of Iceland, more than 60 percent of Icelanders either believe in elves or believe that the existence of elves is possible. A mere 13 percent completely discount the notion that they share their island homeland with the magical, mercurial creatures.

The fantastical landscape is a suitable place for elves. Continental plates meet here, Europe on one side, America on the other. Thermal pools hiss and bubble and occasionally explode. Waterfalls tumble. In the unsettled interior, there are no villages and few visitors, except for the horseback riders who annually ride into the mountains to collect the horses and sheep that have been grazing free all summer. Hikers explore the area on foot, but the elves seem to avoid foreigners. That doesn't mean they aren't there: perhaps before you can meet the mystical creatures, you have to speak the language.

Easier said than done. Just look at the place names on the Laugavegurinn Trail, Iceland's most popular long walk, which crosses a southern slice of Iceland from the thermal springs area of Landmannalaugar to the glacial valley of Þórsmörk, named after Thor the Norse god of thunder. (The Icelandic letter Þ more or less equates to Th in the Roman alphabet.) As you hike, you might stay at the Hrafntinnusker, Álftavatn, Hvanngil, or Emstrur Refuges, take a side trail to dramatic Markarfljótsgljúfur Canyon, or gaze up at Eyjafjallajökull. And just try to pronounce *that*—scores of television news announcers twisted their tongues as they reported about the 2010 volcano that spewed enough ash to stop European air traffic (not to mention damage towns and villages, threaten both humans and livestock, and shut down the hiking route).

Iceland is one of the world's most geothermally active land masses, and one of the least densely populated countries. Much of its interior is wilderness—uninhabited (unless you count the elves). In this rocky, volcanic arctic-desert, the silence can be overwhelming—not merely the absence of sound, but the presence of an anti-sound so profound that it has a weight and gravity of its own. Until the wind howls.

It is also full of surprises: you can scuba dive in glacial melt-off or ride a window washer's cage into the interior of a dormant volcano. But perhaps the biggest surprise is that parts of it are so green while other parts are so lifeless and barren you might think you are hiking on the moon. The green is not because of forests—the wind and cold stunt tree growth so completely that Icelanders joke that if you get lost in an Icelandic forest you should simply stand up. The land is instead covered with mosses and grasses that lie like a soft mohair blanket, their shining green contrasting sharply against the colorful rhyolite mountains and the super-saturated blue waters of the creeks and rivers. But where volcanic debris is still new, the green gives way to a harsher palette of grays, blacks, browns, and yellows. Bubbling mud pools, steam vents, and hot springs (those on the trail are too hot for bathing) are reminders that the earth here is volatile.

There are two options for hiking the Laugavegurinn Trail: the classic route, which is 34 miles, goes from Landmannalaugar to Þórsmörk and takes three to four days. A longer alternative begins the same way, but adds on the 13.6-mile Fimmvörduháls Trail from Þórsmörk to Skógar, near the coast. This extension passes between

Rhyolite Hills,
Laugavegurinn Trail

Eyjafjallajökull and the Mýrdalsjökull Glacier, which are as scenic as they are unpronounceable, making for a hike of 48 miles. All three starting and ending points—Landmannalaugar, Þórsmörk, and Skógar—are reachable by bus during the summer. No matter which hike you choose, go southbound from Landmannalaugar: you'll have gravity and elevation on your side, though the first day starts with a hefty climb.

The huts along the route are basic mountain refuges, not catered hostels. Hikers bring their own sleeping bags and food. Stoves, cooking pots, dishes, and utensils are provided for hut guests; campers must bring their own cooking gear. About 100 people a day start the Laugavegurinn Trail during the summer, so huts tend to book up months in advance. Huts usually open around June 25 and close at the beginning of September, but those dates can change if weather conditions are bad. Camping is allowed near the huts but not within designated nature reserves. If you plan to camp, you'll need a tent designed to withstand strong winds.

Iceland's weather is famously unstable. Freezing rain and thick fog in the middle of summer are par for the course, and Icelanders will cheerfully tell you that there is "no such thing as bad weather, only bad clothing." But bad weather here is not simply a minor inconvenience that blocks the views; it can be life-threatening. On average, a hiker dies here every other year.

One of the most common problems is route finding. The trail is well marked, usually with posts stuck in the ground, but fog can descend quickly and obliterate the view from one marker to the next. On hard ground, hikers can usually follow the trail's indentations in the earth. But on snowfields, the footprints of previous hikers quickly melt and refreeze into a featureless surface. Exacerbating the problem is the fact that the distance between posts is greater than it is on dry ground: the next post may be on the other side of a snowfield, not visible when the fog drops. Add freezing rain, cold temperatures, and exhaustion to the equation, and the trek can quickly turn dangerous.

Hikers should be familiar with foul-weather hiking skills: how to pitch a tent in the rain, how to effectively dress in layers, and how to stay warm in cold, wet, and windy conditions. Navigation skills with a map, compass, and GPS are essential. You can get necessary

Hiker along
Laugavegurinn Trail

waypoints at each hut. Although the highest elevation on the trail is only around 3,500 feet, the latitude makes it the equivalent of reaching 10,000 feet in the Alps, so you'll need head-to-toe rain gear, extra fleece layers, a hat, and gloves (even in summer). Several Iceland-based manufacturers make no-nonsense high-tech clothing suitable for the conditions here.

Other challenges include mud, slick footway, a few stretches where cables and ropes are involved, and many frigid streams and rivers that must be forded: depending on rain and snowmelt, they can range from a trickle to a torrent. Avoid the narrow places, where the water runs deepest.

This is a wilderness trail, a mountain trail, and a tundra trail, but most of all it is a tectonic trail through an infant land that is still being shaped. The evidence of the power beneath the surface surrounds you: roaring hot springs, weird and twisted rock formations, vertical canyons, and the volcanic rubble that can stretch for miles. There is a sense of the formidable under-earth violence of jousting continental plates, the above-ground relentlessness of crackling glaciers, the fierceness of Arctic storms.

As you walk among the rocks and boulders, past the still-active volcanoes, the shifting glaciers, and the trembling ground, keep a sharp eye: rocks and boulders may be merely rocks and boulders. Or they may be dwelling places for the elves, who are sometimes thought to represent a balance of power between these forces, and a connection with the land. Tread gently. It would be a good thing to have them on your side.

Þórsmörk,
Laugavegurinn Trail

OPPOSITE
Skogarfoss,
Laugavegurinn Trail

SUPERIOR TRAIL

United States

As far as hiking destinations are concerned, the North Country of Minnesota is unassuming. The optimistically named Sawtooth Mountains (not to be confused with the Idaho range of the same name) rarely top out above 2,000 feet. Climbs, necessarily, are measured in hundreds of feet, not thousands.

This is a horizontal landscape: fields, forests, and, of course, the long shoreline of Lake Superior, sometimes known, without irony, as the Minnesota Riviera. At 350 miles long and 150 miles wide, Lake Superior is the largest lake in the world measured by surface area—truly a freshwater ocean inland. It is also part of an inland corridor of shipping routes that reaches all the way to the Atlantic Ocean via the Great Lakes to the east and the Saint Lawrence Seaway. For hikers, this means an unexpected midwestern experience: watching great ships making their way to the inland port city of Duluth and visiting lighthouses and museums that tell the story of the many shipwrecks that lie below the surface.

This world of shipping, north-country forests, and gentle contours houses a world-class hiking trail. Starting in Duluth, Minnesota, and ending just shy of the US border with Ontario, Canada, the Superior Hiking Trail follows ridges close to the Lake Superior shoreline for approximately 300 miles. It ranges in elevation from 600 feet at the shoreline to 1,800 feet on the hills around Jackson Lake. A designated national recreation trail, the Superior Trail is also an adjunct to the National Scenic Trails System as an alternate route on the North Country Trail. It adds mileage to what is already the nation's longest national scenic trail, but allows long-distance hikers to take advantage of its exceptional lakeshore scenery. Views include the Apostle Islands to the south and Isle Royale to the north, with occasional opportunities to glimpse the Michigan-Wisconsin shoreline far in the distance.

Falls along Saint Louis River,
Jay Cooke State Park

This is a glaciated landscape: the underlying rock was created from magma from much older volcanic eruptions, but the sculpting of the landforms we see today was the work of the glaciers. Today water continues to shape the land as it pours through countless creeks and waterfalls, draining into the lake. As the trail follows the ridges overlooking the lake, it descends into the valleys of these many streams and creeks, and then climbs back up again. This may not be mountain terrain, but there are scores of 100-, 200-, and 300-foot climbs, in and out of canyons and up and around cliffs.

The distinct ecosystems of different forest types—paper birch, quaking aspen, white pine, white fir, spruce, balsam, and cedar—as well as open grasslands and rocky outcroppings with sweeping views, add variety to the experience. So does the wildlife: sightings might include moose and deer, black bears, coyotes, and wolves (the last two more often heard than seen). And while beavers may or may not be seen, their work is everywhere in the form of massive dams. On one such dam, hikers walk across on a 440-foot-long boardwalk.

OPPOSITE

Trail crossing an old beaver dam near Finland, Minnesota

View of Lake Superior from the Superior Hiking Trail

The Superior Trail is a relatively new trail. Inspired by the success of the Appalachian Trail, construction began in the mid-1980s. Like the AT, it is a nonmotorized footpath—no vehicles, no bicycles, no horses. It is also well marked, with plentiful free campsites and trailheads usually spaced five to 10 miles apart, making it ideal for day hikers. The main hiking season is April through late October, although snowshoeing is becoming increasingly popular on some sections. Spring brings the welcome light green of new leaves, but blackflies and mosquitoes are worse during and immediately after the snowmelt. Summer features blackberries and blueberries and welcome dips in the refreshingly cold rivers, lakes, and waterfalls, but also brings humidity. Autumn is a favorite hiking (and also hunting) season

Superior Hiking Trail
through birch forest

OPPOSITE
Superior Hiking Trail
ascending Wolf Rock

for those who can get away: the humidity drops, the bugs have finally departed, hawks and eagles migrate through the region, and the leaves change to brilliant hues of orange, yellow, and red that are reflected in the complementary cobalt waters.

The trail is actually split into two subdivisions: the short Duluth section of about 41 miles, and the North Shore section, which runs 269 miles (plus connectors to trailheads) from Duluth to Canada. The Duluth section is used only by day hikers; no campsites are available. Thru-hiking the trail generally refers to hiking the North Shore section. Some hikers extend their journeys by connecting to the 65-mile Border Route Trail, or go even farther, by adding on the 41-mile Kekekabic Trail to the Boundary Waters Canoe Area. The Superior Hiking Trail Association offers a series of organized hikes of varying lengths, led by naturalists, geologists, photographers, and historians.

Perhaps one of the great advantages of the Superior Trail is precisely that it is off the beaten path. The burgeoning interest in long-distance hiking is bringing hikers into popular marquee destinations at alarming rates: in 2015, Mount Rainier National Park had to curtail its application process for Wonderland Trail permits because it was overwhelmed by applications. Many wilderness areas are implementing permit processes and quotas at popular trailheads. And to relieve the pressure of too many hikers starting at one time in one place, in 2015 the Appalachian Trail Conservancy started promoting thru-hiking in different directions and on a different schedule than is traditional. But on the Superior Trail, campsites remain blessedly reservation- and permit-free, the number of hikers is smaller than on many other world-class trails, and the experience can almost be called "retro." At least for now.

This is a trail about a lakeshore, and the forest that surrounds it, but most of all it is a trail about the North Country. Even in summer, there is always an essence of northerliness here, an ineffable combination of the piney scent of conifers, the forest floor redolent of fallen leaves and mosses, the damp tannin of shaded forest creeks. And there is that slight edge of evening chill even after a warm day, something to remind hikers that summers here are never very long—and that a good way to enjoy them is to be right here, on this trail.

WALES COAST PATH

 *Wales*

Ceredigion Coast Path, part
of the Wales Coast Path,
along Cardigan Bay

OPPOSITE
Wales Coast Path
near Saint Davids

Driving from Queensferry, in the north of Wales, to Chepstow, in the south, via the M5 and M6 is a journey of approximately 180 miles. Figure three hours.

Or you can take the long way via the Llwybr Arfordir Cymru, otherwise known as the Wales Coast Path—an 870-mile footpath that follows as closely as possible the meandering coastline of Wales. Officially opened in May 2012, the Wales Coast Path is one of the newest long-distance walking paths in the world, and—at least until the proposed England Coastal Path opens in 2020—the only hike in the world that follows almost all of its nation's coastline.

To turn a distance of 180 miles into an 870-mile hike takes a great deal of winding, turning, and meandering. The walking path from Queensferry to Chepstow is a long, indirect horseshoe, and the coastline itself is no swath of straight sand beaches, but rather a jigsaw of cliffs, crags, beaches, waterfalls, estuaries, and marshes. An endless series of detours, sometimes several miles long, meander in and out of estuaries in order to cross the rivers that pour into the Irish Sea.

But it is this ragged, zigzagging topography that has made the Wales Coast Path one of the British Isles' scenic highlights and tourism magnets. Earning honors in "best of" destination lists from Lonely Planet and National Geographic, the wild coastal views are accompanied by a wide variety of flora and fauna, especially shorebirds. The trail passes through 11 national nature reserves, two national parks, three designated "areas of outstanding natural beauty," and 23 sites on the Register of Historic Landscapes, as well as colorful fishing villages, market towns, and Cardiff—Wales's capital city.

The idea for a Welsh national coastal path came from a desire to encourage visitors and locals alike to experience the coastline, but there was also an economic motivation. Existing walking routes such as the Pembrokeshire Coast Path National Trail and the Isle of Anglesey Coastal Path were making enormous contributions to the Welsh tourism economy, and planners hoped that development of a path linking the entire coastline would increase the economic benefits of coastal tourism.

For trail planners, linking together bits and pieces of walking paths, roads, private property easements, and trails through public land is usually an excruciating process; many of the world's great long trails have taken decades to build because of land- and easement-acquisition issues. But the Wales Coast Path was

implemented with astonishing speed, perhaps because some of the paths to be included in the system already existed, and perhaps because of commitments and financing provided by government agencies. Whatever the reason, it took a mere six years for the project to link the established paths that already existed in Pembrokeshire, Anglesey, Gwynedd, Ceredigion, and the North Wales Coast and to develop the needed new paths in the trail's three other sections. To date, approximately 75 percent of the walk is on footpaths, with the remaining 25 percent on lightly used country roads; trail managers continue to work on routing the trail as close to the coastline as is safe and practical.

This is not a wilderness trail, although there is a feeling of wildness in the ocean air: the calls of seabirds, the pounding of the waves, the wind, and the bite of Atlantic air. But the trail is usually within a short distance of towns and roads, making it accessible for casual users, and giving long-distance hikers the option of easy resupply. As with any long trail, long-distance and multiday hikers come from all over the country and abroad. But the trail was also designed to be accessible to walkers of all ages, fitness levels, and abilities. As a result, it is popular with locals as well as tourists. Some sections are especially designated for multiple recreation uses and are suitable for cyclists, families with baby carriages, people with restricted mobility, and horseback riders; other sections, usually through private land, have too many gates and stiles for anything but walking to be practical.

For hikers who want an even longer hike, the Wales Coast Path can be linked with the Offa's Dyke Path, which loosely follows the border with England, to create a 1,030-mile-long continuous walking route around almost the whole of Wales. Or they can wait until 2020, the planned opening date for the new 2,600-mile England Coastal Path and add the two together for a monumental 3,670-mile journey.

COAST TO COAST WALK

England

Black Sail Hut, Lake
District National Park

OPPOSITE
17th-century Smardale
Bridge, Coast to Coast Walk

The English system of national trails includes 16 long-distance paths that cross virtually every ecosystem in the country, along with a variety of cultural, historic, and social settings. So it is interesting that perhaps the best known of England's long-distance walks is not an official national trail, but a largely unsignposted walking route that began as the suggestion of a hiker. Alfred Wainwright's Coast to Coast Walk is so strongly associated with the hiker himself that the trail is often referred to simply by his name—the Wainwright route. Wainwright himself called it "a coast to coast route," the tiny indefinite article making an important point: that there are many ways hikers can create their own routes. Nonetheless, Wainwright's path has achieved worldwide recognition, and whether a national trail or not, it is one of England's signature walks.

Starting on the Irish Sea coastline at Saint Bees and ending in the town of Robin Hood's Bay on the North Sea, the 192-mile trail passes some of northern England's most beloved scenery, including three very different national parks: the Lake District National Park, the Yorkshire Dales National Park, and the North York Moors National Park.

The landscape reveals an essential difference between the North American and European conceptions of wildness, open space, trails, and national parks. England is, of course, both much smaller and much more densely populated than the United States (660 people per square mile versus 85 people per square mile; 104 people per square mile if you exclude Alaska and Hawaii). So it is not surprising that its wildness seems more contained. A cluster of trees that the English call a forest may seem little more than a copse to North American eyes, and there is certainly no possibility that one might round a bend in the trail and find oneself face to face with a bear or a moose.

The numbers are also modest: all of the peaks in England above 3,000 feet are in the Lake District, including England's 3,209-foot high point, Scafell Pike. The high point on Wainwright's route is a mere 2,560 feet at Kidsty Pike. But as experienced hikers know, numbers don't tell the whole story: the conditions are harsh enough that UK mountain rescue teams are kept busy dealing with lost and injured hikers, many of whom make the mistake of overconfidence and underpreparation. Fog can move in. Ridges can be steep with precipitous

dropoffs. And when storms roll in from the Atlantic, the weather can change in the time it takes to realize you've lost sight of the next trail marker or cairn.

Yet it is often not far to safety, if, that is, you can find your way through the fog. The mountains are settled, divided into patchworks by ancient stone walls. The national parks contain not only mountains, lakes, and rivers, but towns where people live. This is not wilderness in the grand, untrammeled sense, but wildness amid settlement; nature surrounding history and culture. The trail has a sense of balance. The result is a walk that compresses a little bit of everything English into a two- to three-week holiday.

The Coast to Coast Walk follows public rights of way including footpaths, country lanes, and mountain roads, some of which have been in use since Roman times. The recommended route has changed several times since its inception in 1973 to avoid trespassing, high-traffic areas, erosion, and other problems of long-distance trail routing. Additionally, guidebooks suggest alternate routes, either to avoid seasonal issues like mud and erosion; to give walkers a choice between easier lowland routes and more challenging, wild upland routes; or to offer a safer passage in bad weather.

The guidebook suggests a practical itinerary of 12 overnight stops, each at a town along or near the trail, but that makes for challenging mileage and elevation on some of the stages. More relaxed itineraries are possible. Hikers do not have to carry tents: towns are conveniently spaced for inn-to-inn hiking, and several local companies will transport luggage from one stage to the next. Accommodations range from bed-and-breakfasts to inns to pubs, each offering the chance to meet fellow hikers, buy meals and drinks, clean up, sleep comfortably, and carry a lighter pack.

Most walkers head in an eastbound direction, starting at Saint Bees, with the prevailing winds (and attendant rains) at their backs. Wainwright suggests a little ritual: that hikers dip their toes in the waters of the Irish Sea to mark the beginning of their journey.

The walk commences with several miles of dramatic cliff-top trail heading north along the coast. Crossing the West Cumbrian coastal plain, the path climbs into the Lake District. Despite the frequent town visits and almost paltry-sounding elevations, there is a sense of drama here that seems entirely out of scale. The daily routine mostly consists of long climbs in the morning, followed by long descents in the afternoon, with several ups and downs in between. The mountains have a cold bite about them. Navigating can be difficult: the trail is deliberately undermarked here in order to preserve the sense of wildness, but this requires hikers to carry the most recent guidebook along with maps, a compass, and a GPS. It should go without saying that hikers should also be able to use this equipment to find their way in thick fog or through a maze of tracks worn through the mud. The occasional giant cairns found atop some of the peaks can appear as sentries or saviors, giving needed assurance about one's location or direction—or both.

Leaving the Lake District, the trail enters its central section where it crosses the Pennine Way, one of England's best-known official national trails. Climbing to the country's main east-west divide brings hikers into a region of highland streams and moors, and Yorkshire Dales National Park.

The final, easternmost section of trail begins near Richmond with some flattish farmlands, then climbs to the North York Moors National Park, the last of the national parks on its route. Here it joins another national trail, the Cleveland Way, which leads through moors that seem like something out of *Wuthering Heights*. The walk ends, finally, on another cliff overlooking another sea. At the end point in the town of Robin Hood's Bay, Wainwright suggests that hikers dip their toes in the North Sea to mark the completion of their journey.

They can also sign a trail register at Robin Hood's Bay, where previous hikers have made a few notes and comments. Thumbing through an old register, you might come upon a cheeky American's invitation to British fellow walkers: "We've done yours. Now come do ours."

Overlooking the North Sea near Robin Hood's Bay

DIVERSITY AROUND THE WORLD

Abel Tasman Track,
New Zealand

OPPOSITE
Bruce Trail, Canada

Abel Tasman Track, New Zealand

One of the easiest, prettiest, and most relaxing coastal trails in the world, the 37-mile Abel Tasman Track follows the northern coastline of New Zealand's South Island. Most hikers take three to five days for the trip, and sleep in huts or camp on the beach. Take lunch breaks while watching the surf, and then hike across wide tidal flats (you'll need to time some crossings for low tide). Look for seals or penguins, and then follow the trail into the lush coastal forests. This is a mild Mediterranean climate, with sun-washed hills covered in chaparral and vineyards. One of New Zealand's Great Walks, the track has four huts and 18 campsites, many of them on the beach.

Bruce Trail, Canada

The Niagara Escarpment is instantly familiar: Niagara Falls plunges over one part of it. But that famous precipice is part of a much larger geological feature. The Bruce Trail, Canada's oldest and longest hiking trail, follows Ontario's section of the Niagara Escarpment for 550 miles from Niagara to Tobermory on the Bruce Peninsula. An additional 155 miles of side trails further explore the region; one of them leads to Niagara Falls. This is a densely populated area, and the trail is popular, so don't expect a wilderness experience. But the escarpment is also a UNESCO World Biosphere Reserve, characterized by two major biomes: boreal needleleaf forests in the north and temperate broadleaf forests in the south. The trail passes through farms, vineyards, recreation areas, cliffs, wetlands, beaches, coastlines, conifer swamps, rolling hills, waterfalls, historic sites, villages, towns, and cities. The biosphere reserve region includes the largest species diversity among Canadian biosphere reserves, with more than 300 bird species, 55 mammals, 36 reptiles and amphibians, and 90 fish.

Lycian Way, Turkey

The Lycian Way takes its name from the ancient civilization that once ruled the mountainous region along the Teke Peninsula in southwestern Turkey. The 335-mile Lycian Way winds around the coast from Ölüdeniz, near Fethiye, to Geyikbayırı, about 12 miles from Antalya. It is blazed with red and white stripes. The route can be walked in winter, although spring and fall (February through May; September through November) have the

most clement weather. Summer is best avoided because of the heat. Coastal views and beaches are a constant here, but high snowcapped peaks can also be seen—there is even the opportunity to climb 7,835-foot Mount Olympos. Daily itineraries feature plenty of short ups and downs as the path veers away from the sea, then returns to it, and the footway, as is typical of trails in the Mediterranean, is often stony and sun baked. There's also an interesting cultural element in the ruins of ancient Lycian cities, historic sites such as castles and lighthouses, and quaint villages where hikers can stop for meals and accommodations. Camping is permitted.

Ice Age Trail, United States

Wisconsin's 1,200-mile Ice Age Trail is America's only national scenic trail devoted to a geological event. It follows the line of the terminal moraine from the Wisconsinan glaciation during the last Ice Age. Starting in Door Peninsula, one of the state's top outdoor recreation areas, it arcs first south, then north, then west around the state to end at the Saint Croix River on the border with Minnesota. Highlights include an abundance of geological formations—kettles, moraines, eskers, drumlines, kames, and erratics—caused by the movement and melting of the enormous mile-deep ice sheet that one covered most of Canada and the northern United States. The best time to hike is summer and fall.

Florida Trail, United States

The 1,400-mile Florida Trail is the continental United States' only subtropical trail, and as such, it offers the unique opportunity to explore a junglelike landscape without all of the challenges of hiking in the tropics, especially in winter, which is characterized by mild temperatures and relatively little rain. A highlight of the trail is its southernmost section along the Big Cypress National Preserve, one of America's most unusual habitats—a 40-mile-wide river that is between a few inches to a few feet deep. It's challenging wet-footed hiking, but the sawgrass prairies and cypress stands are biologically rich. The Ocala National Forest, the Aucilla Sinks, and the UWF Dunes Preserve along the Gulf of Mexico showcase completely different aspects of a state whose ecology is unique in the United States.

Lycian Way, Turkey

FOLLOWING SPREAD
Ice Age Trail, Wisconsin, United States (top left);
Florida Trail, Florida, United States (bottom left);
Arizona Trail, Arizona, United States (right)

Arizona Trail, United States

From the Mexican border near Coronado National Monument to the Utah border north of the Grand Canyon, the 800-mile Arizona Trail takes in everything from the saguaro cactus of the Sonoran Desert to pinyon-juniper forests to the jagged mountains of the Santa Rita, Santa Catalina, and San Francisco Mountains to the Grand Canyon itself. This is a wide, large landscape, with an abundance of ecological diversity. The best time to hike is spring, although if you don't mind cold temperatures and occasional snow, most of the trail can be hiked in winter. The Arizona Trail was added to the National Scenic Trails System in 2011.

Otter Trail, South Africa

Named for the native Cape clawless otter, the Otter Trail begins at the Storms River Mouth at Tsitsikamma, South Africa's adventure capital, where it is possible to do everything from scuba diving to ziplining. From here, it is 25 miles to the trail's end at Nature's Valley. The trail is an easy five-day hike, with daily hiking times ranging from two to six hours, and reserved overnights at four huts. Reservations must be made in advance. Tsitsikamma National Park protects 50 miles of coastal mountains, forests, and beaches; the entire trail is within its boundaries. The coastal views are a unifying theme of the hike, but the trail frequently descends steeply to beaches or river crossings, and then climbs back up to the cliffs overlooking the Indian Ocean. When you're finished, take a side trip to Bloukrans River Gorge, site of the highest bungee jump in the world.

Kalalau Trail, United States

Following Kauai's remote Nā Pali Coast, the Kalalau Trail was once the route used by native Hawaiians to access grazing lands. Today, it is the only way to experience the unique fingerlike cliffs, or palis, that plunge into the ocean. The trail is short—a 22-mile round trip—but strenuous and not suited for hikers with acrophobia: at times, it seems that the path is determined to slide over the edge of the cliffs and down to the sea. Ocean views unfold as you wind up and over the colorful palis. The trails starts at Keʻe Beach, at the road's end beyond Hanalei, and climbs up, beginning a series of climbs and

Otter Trail, South Africa

FOLLOWING SPREAD
Kalalau Trail, Hawaii,
United States

GREAT HIKING TRAILS OF THE WORLD

descents that end at Kalalau Beach. Camping is only permitted on the beach at Hanakoa Valley (at the six-mile mark) and at Kalalau Beach. The combination of falls and drownings have put this hike on several "most dangerous" lists; be extremely cautious when walking on muddy or slick trails, and respect the dangerous tides and ocean currents. More people drown at Hanakapi'ai Beach, a popular day-hiking destination just two miles from the trailhead at Ke'e Beach, than at any other beach on Kauai.

East Coast Trail, Canada

The 340-mile East Coast Trail alternates between showing off the dramatic wilderness geography of Newfoundland's Atlantic Coast, while highlighting some of the culture and history to be found along the way. The coastal wilderness features a traverse atop seaside cliffs that plummet to a roaring ocean: hikers will see "the Spout" (a natural water spout created by wave action), coastal barachois (lagoon) formations, towering cliffs, fjords, headlands, beaches, sea stacks, rock arches, waterfalls, and icebergs floating past. Wildlife includes seabird colonies, humpback whales, and the world's southernmost caribou herds. Historic sites of interest include two active archaeological digs, abandoned settlements, lighthouses, a 164-foot suspension bridge, and coastal communities. About 165 miles of trail are currently complete with maps and signage (most of the way from Cape Saint Francis to Cappahayden). The remaining 171 miles are not yet marked; only experienced backcountry hikers with good route-finding skills should attempt the unfinished segments. While this is mostly a summer-use trail, some sections close to towns are popular snowshoeing routes for day-trippers in the winter.

Great Ocean Walk, Australia

Wombats, wallabies, kangaroos, koalas, and kookaburras will be your companions along this 65-mile hike in southeastern Australia's bush and beach landscapes. So might ants, bees, European wasps, and leeches—as well as tiger, brown, and copperhead snakes, all of which are on *Australian Geographic*'s list of the 10 most dangerous snakes in Australia. The trail's ecology is nothing if not diverse. The Great Ocean Walk teeters on the edge of high cliffs, descends to beaches from which you might see whales in June through September, then turns into coastal forests as it makes its way from Apollo Bay to Glenample Homestead, located near the Twelve Apostles, a famed set of limestone seastacks. Seven hike-in campsites are spaced six to 10 miles apart; the walk takes about eight days to complete and campsites must be reserved in advance. The hike is also noted for its historic sites, many of which tell the stories of shipwrecks (and lighthouses built to help prevent them). Going back about 105 million years earlier, there is a section called the Otways known for dinosaur fossils.

East Coast Trail, Canada

OPPOSITE
Great Ocean Walk, Australia

CHAPTER 6

The LONGEST WALKS

To get lost in the woods of the Appalachian Trail. To connect with the wild on the Pacific Crest Trail. To walk across the entire continent of Europe. To traverse the islands of New Zealand or the Australian Outback—on foot. • What would it be like, one wonders, to throw off the shackles of everyday life—routine, family, work, obligations, bills, ambition—and simply walk, with nothing more to do than watch as the landscape unfolds under your feet? • The magic of a thru-hike lies in the very definition of what a long-distance trail is: a recreational resource that is built for everyone, that showcases and connects communities and ecosystems over a long distance, and that provides an opportunity for extraordinary journeys. • Why walk? Edmund Hillary's answer about mountains translates well to a long-distance trail: because it's there. • What exactly do hikers expect to find on a six-month journey, where they struggle under heavy loads while

walking 15, 20, 25 miles a day, day after day? The beauty of the outdoors is a constant companion, but you don't need to walk 2,000 miles to find a beautiful mountain to climb. And the challenges can be overwhelming: route finding, exhaustion, physical injuries, bugs, mountains that seem to have no end, and the unrelenting battle with the elements, including rain and snow, heat and cold, fierce winds, fog, and humidity.

Yet this idea of a long walk, a journey that combines challenge, escape, nature, adventure, and some unbelievably, unattainably long distance, resonates—a romantic notion. Epic, even. Until, that is, one steps out onto the trail and confronts the day-to-day realities of on-trail life, which, upon close inspection, do not seem romantic or epic at all.

You get up, eat breakfast, strike camp, start walking. Stop to rest, walk, stop to eat, walk, stop to rest, walk, stop for the night. Make camp, eat. Go to sleep with the sun. The complexities of the modern world and all its choices are reduced to essentials, to a few basic questions, answered one day after the next after the next. Where is the water? How far will I walk? How many mountains will I climb? How will I find my way? Where will I stop to sleep?

At the core of this epic adventure is a simple lifestyle that comes as almost a sigh of relief. In a society that sometimes seems to have too much of everything, hiking a long trail is one experience that is determinedly old-fashioned. Even technology doesn't make it much easier. Our gear may be lighter, our clothing more functional, our information more accurate and accessible (until, that is, our mobile devices lose their signals and turn into dead weight). But with or without technology, the main difficulty of putting one foot in front of the other remains something we have in common with the very first humanoids who walked out of Africa.

The engagement in the predictable daily routine creates the unique personal journey each hiker experiences on a long-distance trail. A thru-hike is never just about the destination; it is also about the journey—something pilgrims have been learning for more than 1,000 years as they navigate the stages on the path to enlightenment: breaking in, learning skills, beginning to feel competent, and, finally, becoming fully at home in their new world. The same stages apply to any thru-hiker, on any trail.

We begin with question marks. What kinds of physical obstacles will be encountered? What kinds of communities of people? Will the trails be well blazed or barely marked? And, above all, this question: Can I do it?

The journey holds the answers.

But as much as a long-distance hike is a personal quest, it is also a travel experience. Long trails cross vast amounts of territory—hundreds, sometimes thousands of miles—and as they change latitude and elevation, they cross strikingly different ecosystems and cultural zones. The Pacific Crest Trail in the American West traverses six of America's major ecozones. Europe's GR5 meanders not only through the different ecozones of Western Europe—the below-sea-level flatlands of Holland; the rolling hills, forests, and farmlands of Belgium and Luxembourg; the river valleys of the Rhineland; the low mountains of the Vosges; the high mountains of the Alps; and the dry Mediterranean Coast—but also traverses a similar variety of human cultures, passing through cities, towns, and villages with war memorials, vineyards, beer-making monasteries, battlefields, museums, ancient churches, Roman ruins, and ski resorts, painting a picture of the European cultural landscape.

Seeing all this at the walker's pace of two or three miles an hour provides time to absorb the surroundings at a shockingly slow rate: a fraction of a degree of latitude at a time, one footstep of elevation gain followed by the next. The changes are miniscule but also inevitable: cacti give way to pine trees; rattlesnakes no longer bask on rocks, but pikas do. The browns of mud season turn into the light-filled greens of early spring. Days lengthen or shorten. The sun strengthens or weakens. A single leaf on an aspen tree turns yellow; a week later, you find yourself walking through a grove of trees the color of sunlight. The snow starts to fall.

But it is not just long-distance hikers who benefit from long-distance trails. To the contrary, long-distance hikers are only a small minority of worldwide trail users. So what is the difference between hiking a 10-mile section of the Appalachian Trail and some other 10-mile trail? Why should trekkers who have no intention of hiking an entire trail care whether a long-distance trail goes to Maine or Georgia or the other side of Europe?

The specifics vary, but most long-distance trails are designed to offer marquee experiences: in each region,

trail planners try to route them over the most prominent peaks, through the best parks, along the most scenic ridges. Equally important, long trails have supportive, engaged communities. Sometimes this means the trails are better marked and maintained. Sometimes it means there are better guidebooks. Sometimes it means there is enough support for hiker hostels, services such as vehicle shuttles, or guided group hikes for beginners. Sometimes it means that a community exists to lobby for the trail and protect its surrounding environment.

And sometimes it is something much simpler: long-distance trails offer the chance to be part of something grand. When you hike even a short distance on a long trail, you are acutely aware of the potential to keep going: over the next mountain, to the next ridge, across that far horizon. What you do with this awareness is up to you. Perhaps you simply go home, nurse sore muscles, and read a book about it. Perhaps you join a trail club. Or maintain a section of trail. Or plan a long hike of your own.

Mostly, long-distance trails provide a place for us to do what we were born to do: we were born to walk. Forget for a moment all the ways we have found to avoid walking—from chariots to jet planes, donkeys to bullet trains, camels to cars—deep down we know better. We instinctively understand the wisdom of the new catchphrase, "sitting is the new smoking." We buy treadmill desks and walking shoes and magazines filled with 100 ways to walk our way back to health. And some of us hike, and then hike some more, and a small number of us find ourselves crossing an entire country on our own two feet.

Ask a hundred hikers why they are doing it and you'll get a hundred answers. Those answers will touch on all the reasons people have ever walked anywhere: to explore new places, to experience spiritual transformation, to reach the highest places, to learn about different cultures, to discover different ecosystems, to walk for charity or health or bragging rights, to escape, to recover and heal, to take a vacation, to make like-minded friends, to reconnect with wildness.

Walking is among a cluster of attributes that makes humans human. We have large brains, we have opposable thumbs, we use tools, we understand and plan for the future, we bury our dead, we consider the infinite and the possibility of a deity. And we walk.

Pacific Crest Trail,
California, United States

FOLLOWING SPREAD
England Coastal Path,
England

APPALACHIAN TRAIL

United States

Lake Onawa and
Barren Ledges, Maine

OPPOSITE

Appalachian Trail
through Shenandoah
National Park, Virginia

The Appalachian Trail, arguably the most famous long-distance path in the world, was actually not created with long-distance hikers in mind.

Benton MacKaye, the visionary who first proposed the idea of an Appalachian trail, was thinking of an entirely different group of people when he dreamed up the idea of a footpath to run the length of the Appalachian Mountains. MacKaye considered physical exertion in the wilderness a path to sanity in an increasingly urban world. He saw industrialization and the smoky, polluted, soul-destroying cities that went with it as a threat to physical and mental health. MacKaye's idea was to create rural communities and recreational opportunities for respite and rejuvenation—not for quests, conquests, or personal records.

It wasn't until more than 20 years after work on the trail began that the first thru-hiker arrived: in 1948, Earl Shaffer, a veteran of the brutal fighting in World War II's Pacific theater, took to the trail to walk off his wartime memories. It took another 20 years before thru-hikers started coming in any significant numbers. According to Appalachian Trail Conservancy records (which make no distinction between single-season thru-hikers and section hikes completed over a number of years), 14 people completed the trail in the 1950s, 37 in the 1960s, and 775 in the 1970s.

Only in the 1990s did the numbers of end-to-enders (a total of 3,332 throughout the decade) become significant enough to find their way into the popular imagination. Today, some four million people visit the Appalachian Trail each year, perhaps 1,000 of whom complete the entire trail. By far the majority of trail users come for hikes of a few hours, or perhaps a few days.

Located in what was America's first mountain wilderness, the Appalachian Trail has aspects of almost all the key elements that bring walkers to wild places. It is both an accessible and an attractive destination. Located no more than a three-hour drive from most of the major metropolises of the East Coast, much of the trail is remarkably wild. The combination of large tracts of forest and mountains that are accessible to nearby towns for transportation and resupply eases some of the logistical challenges of planning a hiking vacation.

The Appalachians are tired mountains, worn down by time, and long since done with challenging the sky. Topping out under 7,000 feet, they lack the overpowering drama of the big western ranges: there is

no permanent snow on the Appalachian Trail, and few long stretches above tree line. But what the AT lacks in big-mountain majesty, it makes up for with a unique diversity of landscapes, some of which are found nowhere else. The subdued blue ridges of the Great Smoky Mountains are instantly identifiable, as are the rhododendron-covered balds of the Tennessee-North Carolina border. Also instantly identifiable are the rocky ridges of Pennsylvania and the fiercely rugged trails of the White Mountains and western Maine.

In between the mountain landscapes are rural valleys, farmlands, and the forests that give the Appalachian Trail its nickname of "the long green tunnel." In spring, the palette expands to include redbud, dogwood, azalea, and mountain laurel; in autumn, it means blazing foliage in every shade from purple to yellow.

The AT also offers up a variety of sites that showcase different periods in American history. Mountain life is represented in the folk styles of housing and fencing seen along the route. Civil War history surrounds the trail from Virginia to Pennsylvania; the battlefields and memorials at Harpers Ferry, Antietam, and Gettysburg are close enough to the trail to schedule in a visit. In New England, towns proudly proclaim birthdays that make them older than the United States. Popular imagination sometimes says that the Appalachian Trail follows old Native American paths, but unlike so many other hiking paths, the AT actually follows few historic routes of travel, Native American or otherwise: scrambling up and down virtually every mountain to be found is rarely an efficient way to get from here to there, and many of America's historic travel ways went east-west across the mountains. North-south routes sensibly avoided the summits and ridges.

Although thru-hikers are only a small minority of Appalachian Trail hikers, they are a highly visible group, especially at the beginning of the season. Compatible hikers form traveling communities, resembling nothing so much as Chaucer's medieval storytelling pilgrims

Appalachian Trail near
Little Haystack Mountain,
New Hampshire

on their way to Canterbury. Indeed, the Appalachian Trail—which has no associations with formal religious pilgrimage—in many ways resembles the ancient pilgrimages more than the ancient pilgrimages themselves. Today's pilgrimage to Santiago de Compostela can be done on a bicycle, and all a pilgrim has to do to earn the revered *compostela* is walk a mere 62 miles. To get the certificate from the Appalachian Trail Conservancy requires walking 2,180 miles—more than 30 times as far.

Like the ancient pilgrimages, a thru-hike of the AT is a months-long affair, a physical journey with a spiritual component—although in the case of some AT hikers, that spiritual component may be at first unintended and little understood. But as the ancient pilgrims knew, walking day after day through nature becomes a spiritual process, whether intended or not. And then there is the aspect of community and the traditions and rituals that community creates. Birth names are dropped in favor of trail names in a bonding process that rebirths the hiker as part of the new community, and allows, if only for a time, a break with the old. Some hikers, hoping to interact on their own terms without the baggage that comes with being known as a doctor, a high school dropout, or even (as has happened) a criminal, manage to hike the entire trail without revealing their real names or discussing their professions.

Other parallels pile on. Like the *albergues* of the Spanish pilgrimage, hostel owners welcome hikers, offering cheap beds and meals. So-called trail angels offer rides and help to stranded hikers, perhaps for the same reason that residents along Japan's Shikoku Pilgrimage offer small gifts and encouragement. And, as happens along all the major pilgrimage routes, the discussion of the rules of the journey goes on and on, as hikers try to sort out who is doing it right, what it means to do it right, who is cheating, and whether or not anyone cares.

On the AT many of those discussions take place in trail shelters that are spread along the route, each a day's walk—or less—from the last. The AT is one of the few trails in the United States to have a trail shelter system, although during the high season, hikers need to bring tents because shelter space is limited. The AT has other amenities that endear it to hikers, especially beginners: it's marked so conscientiously with its signature white blazes, precisely two inches by six, that if you walk more than a couple of minutes without seeing one, you can assume that somehow you missed a turn. Map and compass skills are rarely used. Loads don't have to be heavy: every few days, and sometimes even more frequently, there is an opportunity to go off trail to a nearby town to resupply.

All of the foregoing—the community, the shelters, the blazes, the information available, the accessibility—leads prospective long-distance hikers to gravitate to the Appalachian Trail for their first thru-hiking experience. The logic is obvious: lower mountains, a more settled and populated environment, fewer extremes of ecology and climate, more shelters, an established long-distance culture, and plenty of information suggests that the trail will be somehow easy. It is a completely logical conclusion. It is also completely wrong.

"Easy" is in the eye of the beholder: some hikers find going downhill more difficult than going uphill; some hikers find road walking fast and easy while others find it punishing and painful. But however you look at it, physically, there is nothing easy about the Appalachian Trail. It is characterized by a defiant habit of going straight up and down every mountain, hill, or hillock it can find, leading thru-hikers to invent the term PUDs— "pointless ups and downs"—to describe a day filled with small but grueling grinds to viewless summits. Large or small, the elevation changes are relentless: the trail gains (and loses) about 515,000 feet of elevation in its course of nearly 2,200 miles. The profile map is more erratic than a stock market graph.

Yet, at the same time, almost anyone can do it. The oldest person to thru-hike the AT was 81; the youngest was five. The trail has been hiked by families, by several blind hikers, by hikers walking barefoot, even by an amputee using a prosthetic leg; it has been hiked by people hoping to walk off an addiction, a divorce, the passing of a loved one, the loss of a job, or the horrors of war. The community in this wilderness, this rollicking band of modern-day pilgrims, comprises every age, social class, profession, and level of education. Hiking the Appalachian Trail may be about the best way there is to discover America and Americans—not only the hikers, but the local residents, trail angels, trail maintainers, and volunteers, all of whom have made a place in their lives for this thin ribbon that ties together all of the lands and peoples from Maine to Georgia.

Annapolis Rocks, Maryland (top left); Amicalola Falls, Georgia (top right); wild ponies in Grayson Highlands, Virginia (bottom left); Appalachian Trail through cornfield near Boiling Springs, Pennsylvania (bottom right)

FOLLOWING SPREAD
Round Bald, Roan Mountain Highlands, North Carolina

PACIFIC CREST TRAIL

United States

The Pacific Crest Trail has historically resided in the long shadow of an older but smaller sibling. Simply put, the Appalachian Trail came first, and with all the advantages of a firstborn, it enjoys an iconic status in the world of long-distance hiking.

But there is room for more than one iconic trail in our collective imagination, and in recent years, the Pacific Crest Trail has stepped up to play its trump card. Trail boosters call it the "Everest of hiking trails." And they have good reason. As the real estate agents say: location, location, location.

The PCT's 2,780-mile-long path from Mexico to Canada traverses most of the pinnacle wildernesses and mountain ranges of the West Coast of the United States. A *New York Times* best-selling memoir and a major motion picture brought the trail into the public spotlight. Having hooked the attention of the outdoors world, the PCT will have no trouble keeping it: with its superb mountain landscape, the trail no longer sits meekly as a western counterpart to a famous sibling from back east. The PCT has come into its own.

And about time, for this is a very different trail—more wild, less peopled, more scenic, less convenient. It has all of the aspects of a great long trail: an element of pilgrimage, mountains, wilderness, other varied landscapes, culture, and history. But the proportions and overall effect are different.

Here, the journey is less about a community of pilgrims traveling together with rituals intact and more about the shrines themselves: the great cathedrals of wilderness that have given America its understanding of what this wilderness means and why it is important. Much of this understanding was honed right here in the lands adjoining the Pacific Crest Trail. Would we even have wilderness without John Muir and Ansel Adams?

The PCT passes through their eponymous wilderness areas, and through other lands they worked to save. The place names are legendary, one after the other: Yosemite and Kings Canyon, the Mojave Desert, Mount Hood, Mount Rainier, Crater Lake, the North Cascades, all—in the words of trail founder Clinton C. Clarke—"strung like pearls, the mountain ranges of Washington, Oregon, and California. The Pacific Crest Trail is the cord that binds this necklace, each gem encased in a permanent wilderness protected from all mechanization and commercialization."

This is a place where the landscape dwarfs everything, including the humans who have sought to cross it, and the history they have left behind. Partly, this is because the trail deliberately avoids areas of settlement. The high mountains are inhospitable for most kinds of development, and many of the ridges along the PCT's route are protected as wilderness. In those areas that have been settled, the local history tells us not heroic tales of how humans imposed their will on the land, but rather stories of hardship. Donner Pass, through which Interstate 80 now passes, reminds us of our vulnerability in the face of nature's wrath. The California Gold Rush mountain towns tell tall tales of nature's immense riches, and the equally immense struggle to claim them. Life on the edge of the Mojave is a scrappy affair, harsh and dusty, as seen in the hardscrabble settlements that serve as town stops for hikers.

It is that enormous and powerful landscape, ultimately, that defines the Pacific Crest Trail. Each of its component parts—its mountains, its deserts, its old-growth forests—is almost a platonic ideal. The mountains of the Sierra define what mountains ought to be; the old-growth forests of northern Washington are the epitome of great trees.

Deep Creek,
Hot Springs, California

An overview of the PCT's landscapes can barely scratch the surface: from south to north, the trail passes through the desertlike mountains of the Laguna, San Jacinto, San Bernardino, and San Gabriel ranges before crossing a spur of the Mojave Desert and climbing into the Tehachapis. That adds up to a journey of four to six weeks, during most of which the hiker will be consumed with thoughts about water: where the next water will be found, how much water to carry, how much is left in a canteen.

The trail's character completely changes in the High Sierra, where thru-hikers usually find themselves navigating snowy passes and raging mountain streams in

Lost Lake, California

OPPOSITE
Descent into Whitewater Canyon, California

one of the world's most pristine mountain wildernesses. Here, the PCT follows the John Muir Trail for nearly 200 miles through Sequoia and Kings Canyon and Yosemite National Parks, passing just below 14,494-foot Mount Whitney (hikers can take a side trip to the summit of this highest point in the contiguous 48 states) before bounding over a series of high passes between 10,000 and 12,000 feet in elevation, each more spectacular than the one before. Later in the summer, this stretch of trail becomes one of the most beloved hiking areas in the United States.

North of Yosemite, the trail continues through the rest of the Sierra before entering the volcanically unstable North Cascades, passing within sight, and sometimes on the slopes of, 11 glaciated cones that line up like sentries: Lassen, Shasta, the Three Sisters, Jefferson, Hood, Saint Helens (off to the side), Adams, Rainier, and Glacier Peak.

The statistics are nothing short of astonishing: according to the Pacific Crest Trail Association, the trail crosses 57 major mountain passes, dips into 19 major canyons, and passes more than 1,000 lakes and tarns. Land units include four national monuments, five state park units, six national parks, seven Bureau of Land Management field offices, 25 national forest units, and 48 federal wilderness areas.

To hike the trail in one season is an enormous challenge. The long length combined with the short snow-free window of the high country forces hikers to maintain a rigorous pace: 20-mile days are common. And to hike in a single season, most thru-hikers encounter some combination of extreme heat in the desert, extreme cold in the mountains, and many miles of sometimes frightening travel on snow and ice. Nonetheless, the number of prospective thru-hikers on the PCT has grown exponentially in recent years, continuing the trend of increasing interest seen since the 1970s, and fueled by recent high-profile media attention.

As with the Appalachian Trail, the vast majority of hikers on the PCT are day hikers or weekenders, followed by those out for journeys of a few days to a few weeks. The trail's location near the metropolises of the West Coast—and in some of the most spectacular national parks and wildernesses of the West—makes it a popular getaway, providing the sort of rejuvenating wilderness respite that is at the heart of the long-distance hiking movement in the United States.

Thousand Island Lake, Ansel Adams Wilderness, California

FOLLOWING SPREAD
Pacific Crest Trail through Mount Hood National Forest, Oregon (left); Tipsoo Lake, Chinook Pass, Washington (top right); pond in Goat Rocks Wilderness, Washington (bottom right)

CONTINENTAL DIVIDE TRAIL

United States

On a relief map of the United States, a jumble of brown bumps fills most of the West. If you look in the middle of that jumble—in New Mexico, Colorado, Wyoming, Idaho, and Montana—you will find a line that snakes from the Mexican border north to Canada. It is not a line of state boundaries, nor international ones (the line continues both south and north of American borders). It is a geographic boundary between east and west: the Continental Divide.

Stand on top of it, face west, and pour some water out from your canteen. The water will fall downslope, and head to the Pacific Ocean. If you face east, the water will go to the Atlantic—at least in theory. In reality, your cup of water will probably puddle into the ground and disappear a few inches beneath your feet. But on a grand scale, if not always visible to the eye, the Continental Divide separates the Atlantic and Pacific Watersheds.

It is both a powerful idea and a powerful reality. During the decades of America's westward exploration and migration, the Continental Divide stood as the great barrier to the West. Carriages, walkers, railroads, roads, tunnels: all had to cross it, and it was never easy. Through most of the 19th century, only two passages allowed for significant routes of travel: the Butterfield Stage Route crossed the Continental Divide in southwestern New Mexico, and the Oregon Trail crossed at South Pass in Wyoming. Today, there are roads and railroads and tunnels, but even so, some of the passes are closed in winter. The Divide remains a formidable obstacle.

Hikers who tackle the Continental Divide Trail from Mexico to Canada hug this intimidating 3,100-mile landmark, sometimes just to the east, sometimes to the west, and sometimes walking right on top of it, challenging the heavens for miles at a time. The Divide runs through five western states, 25 national forests, 21 wilderness areas,

three national parks, one national monument, eight Bureau of Land Management resource areas, and five states—Montana, Idaho, Wyoming, Colorado, and New Mexico. Along with the Appalachian Trail and the Pacific Crest Trail, the Continental Divide Trail is one of the three so-called Triple Crown hiking trails. But it differs from the other two in that it is not yet complete, requiring hikers to do significant amounts of route planning and navigating. (Approximately 75 percent of the trail is considered to be in its more or less permanent location, with another 25 percent following a combination of dirt roads, temporary trails, and cross-country routes.)

Another difference is its remote location: unlike the AT, which is a short drive from many of the East Coast's most populated areas, and the PCT, which is accessible from Seattle, Portland, Sacramento, San Francisco, Los Angeles, and San Diego, the CDT is close only to Denver and Albuquerque. As a result, far fewer people—current estimates are between 150 and 200—attempt thru-hikes of the trail every year. In its more remote sections, day hikers and weekend hikers are few and far between: it is possible to hike a week or more and not see another backpacker.

This is a trail that offers an increasingly rare experience—not only wilderness, but isolation. The John Muir Trail in California—where you can hike for more than a week without seeing a road, a telephone pole, or a place to grab a hamburger and a shower—may be a more complete wilderness experience. But in midsummer, hikers share the JMT's wilderness with hundreds of others. On most of the CDT, you're more likely to cross the occasional road, but less likely to share a campsite.

The Divide also gives hikers plenty of opportunities to ponder the relationship between humans and the mountains. Miners, traders, settlers, and railroad builders did not always move gently on this land, and

Bull moose, Kootenai Lake, Glacier National Park, Montana

FOLLOWING SPREAD
Chimney Rock, Ghost Ranch, New Mexico

the Divide is sometimes littered with the detritus of history. Some, like old mines, excite the imagination: there could still be gold and silver in these hills, untold riches just there for the taking. Other remains, like boom-and-bust mining towns, decrepit and rotting, tell the downside of the same story. On an open stretch in Wyoming's Great Divide Basin, a settler's cabin sits in solitary decay, surrounded by the dusty dun earth under a blazing sky, the only soundtrack a howling wind. What would it have been like to live here? To anchor one's hopes and dreams in such a hostile, unlikely place? Farther north, the Northern Rockies remind us of the early explorers like Jim Bridger, who came this way a mere 200 years ago and brought back tales of landscapes so extreme, so weird, so utterly different that his reports were thought to be myths and fables. "We don't publish fiction" was the acerbic response of one East Coast editor to an article in which Bridger described the wonders of Yellowstone.

Ranging in elevation from 4,200 to 14,200 feet, the Continental Divide Trail crosses a remarkable variety of ecosystems. New Mexico is arid, with long stretches traversing wide-open spaces covered with creosote, mesquite, ocotillo, and the ubiquitous prickly pear. Interrupting the arid drylands are greener higher places like the Gila Wilderness and the San Pedro Parks Wilderness; adding color and variety is the red and gold high-desert landscape of Abiquiu, most famously painted by Georgia O'Keeffe. In Colorado, hikers head straight uphill to the 10,000-foot elevation, and stay there—and higher—for some 700 miles. Colorado's CDT is one of the longest sustained high-country hikes in the world, following endless above-tree-line ridges with views of more and yet more mountains stretching as far as the eye can see. Wyoming's Divide is split into two distinct sections. The southernmost part includes a fierce and dry basin, around which the Continental Divide itself actually splits into two semicircles to form the Great Divide Basin. Hikers usually follow the basin's East Rim to South Pass, where the two prongs of the Divide rejoin. This is where the Oregon Trail settlers, the Mormon immigrants, and the Pony Express crossed the Continental Divide as they made their way to the Willamette Valley in Oregon, California, or Salt Lake City, Utah. The next section includes the spectacularly beautiful Wind River Mountains and Yellowstone

National Park. In Idaho and Montana, the trail is in the Northern Rockies ecosystem, explored by Lewis and Clark. Highlights include the Anaconda-Pintler, Scapegoat, and Bob Marshall Wildernesses, and a grand finale at Glacier National Park. An entire thru-hike needs to be completed in about five to five-and-a-half months in order to fit into the snow-free window.

With the growing interest in long-distance hiking trails and the fact that the Continental Divide offers the chance to backpack through some of America's most dramatic mountain landscapes, it only stands to reason that traffic will continue to increase as the number of thru-hikers from other trails look for new adventures, and as new sections of trail continue to be built. For the moment, though, the CDT is a rarity—still underused and less well known, yet offering an experience that takes hikers into the heart of the western mountain landscape, its variety of ecosystems, and its history.

OPPOSITE
Waterfall in Wind River Range, Wyoming

Trail along Thunderbolt Mountain, Deerlodge National Forest, Montana

The GR5

The Netherlands, Belgium, Luxembourg, Switzerland, and France

Windmill in Heense Molen,
The Netherlands

OPPOSITE
Climb to Col du
Bonhomme, France

Dutch windmills. A chateau in which hikers are invited to stay the night. A World War II concentration camp. The mountain resort of Chamonix. Alsatian vineyards. Lake Geneva. A beach on the French Riviera. The GR5 is a walk through the history and diverse environments of Western Europe: an unmatched combination of cultural sites and outdoor destinations.

The French words *Grande Randonnée* mean "long-distance footpath." Along with similarly designated paths in Belgium, Luxembourg, Spain, Portugal, and the Netherlands, these French paths are part of a network of trails that roam virtually all over Western Europe. France alone has more than 21,000 miles of long-distance hiking trails, all blazed with distinctive red-and-white paint markers along telephone poles, rocks, trees, and signposts. France is only about the size of Texas, and its Grande Randonnée system comprises more miles than the entire National Scenic Trails System of the United States. This is a country that loves to hike.

The 1,500-mile GR5 goes through Holland, Belgium, Luxembourg, and a tiny piece of Switzerland, but it spends most of its time in France. Starting at the North Sea in Hoek van Holland, it ends on the beach at Nice, smack on the French Riviera. It is one of the longest fully-blazed hiking routes in Europe, and also one of the most varied, going from below sea level in the Netherlands to the slopes of Mont Blanc, Western Europe's highest mountain.

The start of the hike is gentle: there aren't many places to climb in Holland, and much of this north-ernmost part of the trail follows bike paths and pleasant trails through local parks, forests, and farmlands, frequently passing through towns. The trail enters Belgium in Dutch-speaking Flanders and leaves it in Francophone Wallonie. History seems a constant companion here: World War II pillboxes sit in forest copses, small-town memorials list the names of the dead, museums commemorate local battles, and place names like the Ardennes are constant reminders of indelible events.

As the trail moves west, the terrain becomes hillier, first in the Ardennes, then in the hills overlooking the rivers of Luxembourg. In France, the Lorraine Plateau gives way to the higher mountains of Alsace, an area of

Franco-German heritage with a complicated history that includes the Stutthof World War II concentration camp, its entrance right on the trail. Continuing through the Jura Mountains, the GR5 enters Switzerland and crosses Lake Geneva (on a ferry, of course), and then heads straight up into the Alps, staying briefly in Switzerland before following the Tour de Mont Blanc for two days. Turning south, the trail continues through the heart of the French Alps, first along the Swiss border, then along the Italian border, where the dry and dramatic Maritime Alps lead down through mountainside villages, vineyards, and fields to the Mediterranean.

The alpine route is strenuous. Rivers drain the French Alps westbound, meaning that the route through the mountains is constantly descending into river valleys and ascending the next pass, with elevations ranging from 1,500 to 10,000 feet. It's not uncommon to gain 4,000 feet of elevation in a day. Enormous variations in ecosystems are caused not only by elevation differences, but also by changes in rainfall, from the gray and rainy north to the rain-shadowed Mediterranean chaparral.

Most hikers take about three-and-a-half months to complete the trip. It is a different sort of hiking than is found on the great American long trails: long-distance backpacking with a European accent. In part, this reflects the differences in landscape. Western Europe is more densely populated, with towns dotting the valleys between mountains and farms and pastures covering the lower slopes. The idea of untracked, uninterrupted wilderness doesn't parse here; instead, the GR5 alternates between civilization and wildness, and most stretches can be hiked without carrying camping equipment, if one is prepared to make reservations and stick to a schedule. In the Alps, the famed system of European mountain huts provides beds and food, although hikers are permitted to camp outside the huts as well, if they prefer.

Languages and cultures change with dizzying frequency. So too do the foods, beers, and wines on offer: local specialties appear and disappear as you pass through the different regions. In Belgium, you might feast on the ubiquitous mussels with *frites*, washed down with one of the country's 500 kinds of beer, perhaps an overproof brew made in a local monastery. In Alsace, the unlikely combination of sauerkraut and fish appears on almost every menu, so you might as well try it (it's

delicious), and pair it with the sweet white wines produced by vintners whose fields you've walked past. In French-speaking Switzerland, it's all about the fondue; farther south, Italian pastas and pizzas start appearing on the menus, and the wine is, by default, red.

Most thru-hikers tackle the trail southbound, perhaps preferring to break in on the easy flats and save the dramatic peaks and the beautiful Mediterranean finale for the end. For hikers not interested in the more populated and less wild northern section, the southern part of the GR5 from Lake Geneva to the Mediterranean is known as the Grand Traverse of the Alps. By far the most popular section is the High Alps region around Chamonix: the popular Tour de Mont Blanc and the Haute Route to Zermatt begin here, and the region is justifiably, internationally, famous. Hikers interested in a more solitary experience might head farther south to the Maritime Alps, which are less well known but every bit as dramatic, although distinctly different, with a drier environment. A southern variant of the GR5 is the GR52, which leads through Mercantour National Park, so remote that it almost feels like a bona fide American wilderness, with high-mountain scenery and few other trekkers.

Taken as a whole, the GR5 may just offer a little bit of every kind of hiking experience imaginable. It certainly competes in the beauty department: the high central Alps have postcard-perfect vistas of mountains and glaciers, interspersed with scores of French *villes de fleurs*, awarded the designation because of their public and private floral displays. Good food (it's France, after all) goes without mention, as does the camaraderie of the high-mountain refuges, where hikers speaking a babel of languages share weather and trail information. Communication is sometimes a challenge for monolingual Americans—there aren't many native English speakers on the trail. But most often, mountain hospitality and good will prevails. The GR5 is an opportunity to experience the vastly different cultures of Western Europe, along with their different histories, cuisines, and environments, ranging from the misty gray shores of the North Sea to the sunny Mediterranean interspersed with some of the world's great mountains. And it is an opportunity to interact with the people, who welcome hikers in Dutch, Flemish, French, Italian, German—and even a little English.

Limestone formation at Hallenbach Stream near Château Beaufort, Luxembourg (top left); near Liège, Belgium (top right); Grandfontaine, Alsace, France (bottom left); Cascade du Rouget, French Alps (bottom right)

FOLLOWING SPREAD
Lac Verte, France (top left); view from Crête des Gittes, France (bottom left); climb to Refuge de Péclet-Polset, France (right)

TE ARAROA

New Zealand

First some language. *Te Araroa* is Māori for "the Long Pathway." A *tramper* is a hiker. A *track* is a trail. A *long-drop* is an outhouse. The *Kiwis* are the residents. And a *friend* is anyone you've interacted with. The rest you can work out as you go.

New Zealand may be the most hiker-friendly country on earth. The variety of trails and environments is unsurpassed. Hiker lodgings are abundant in cities and towns near recreation areas. And on some public bus routes, accommodating drivers will stop at trailheads and wait to be sure they haven't left any hikers behind. Plus, this is one of the few countries where trampers don't have to worry about wild animals, snakes, hiking permits, trail-use quotas, and violence.

It is also one of the most geothermically active places on earth. Formed by the Pacific Ring of Fire, New Zealand's volatile tectonic activity includes earthquakes, volcanoes, and geothermal features such as hot springs, geysers, and steam vents, all of which have created a landscape that is actively changing, sometimes dangerously. In 2011, an earthquake caused enormous damage and killed 185 people in Christchurch on the South Island. In parts of the country earthquakes are weekly occurrences. According to some estimates, there are as many as 15,000 earthquakes in New Zealand each year. Most are minor, but 100 to 150 are strong enough to be felt (although most of them feel like little more than a big truck passing by). Some are much stronger. On Te Araroa in 2011, Mount Tongariro erupted, spewing ash into the sky less than a mile from the famed Tongariro Alpine Crossing.

The climate is as ornery as the forces beneath the ground. Subject to a far-south latitude and an ocean-influenced climate, the weather is frequently unsettled, especially as you move south. This is no place to be

Looking down on Lake Constance from Waiau Pass, Nelson Lakes National Park

experimenting with untested ultralight gear: in some parts of the South Island, a foot of rain can fall in a single day, flooding valley trails thigh high and sometimes more. But that doesn't mean you can forget sunblock, sunscreen, and a sun hat: New Zealand's sunlight is dangerously strong owing to its proximity to Antarctica, where the protective ozone layer is thin.

Te Araroa is one of the world's youngest long-distance footpaths, opened in 2011 by the Te Araroa Trust, which manages the trail. It was created to give walkers a holistic experience of New Zealand—not just its famed coastlines, rain forests, volcanoes, mountain passes, alpine meadows, river valleys, and glacial canyons, but its cities, towns, and farms as well. The track is about 1,900 miles long; the number is currently in flux as relocations change and improve the trailway (usually increasing the mileage). It traverses the entire length of the country, from Cape Reinga on the north tip of the North Island to Bluff at the southern end of the South Island.

New Zealand is not a big country; with only about 104,000 square miles, it is approximately the size of Colorado, and less than half the size of France. But in that space, it manages to cram some of the world's most varied and scenically interesting landscapes, as well as almost shocking transitions in climate and ecosystems. On the north coast of the South Island, hikers can linger on Mediterranean-style chaparral hillsides or stop in vineyards, while on the south side of the same island, they'll find a temperate rain forest that is one of the wettest places on earth. Hikers might share scenic beaches with penguins and seals, then climb into mountain landscapes that can vary from glaciated peaks to stark, still-active volcanic wastelands. Not to mention the farmlands and their 30 million sheep. Approximately 30 percent of New Zealand is protected in parks and reserves that encompass almost all of the country's diverse landforms and ecosystems; 40 percent of the trail crosses conservation land.

Hikers who have experience with New Zealand's well-maintained and graded Great Walks may be surprised if they expect a similar trail standard here: Te Araroa is a much wilder undertaking. While some stretches of trail are easy rambles, trail quality is mixed and often rugged, with boot-sucking mud, slip-sliding scree, tangled vines, prickly shrubs, occasional rock and dirt scrambling, and river crossings that can sweep hikers off their feet during snowmelt or after heavy rains. One section of "trail" has to be covered by kayak (rentals are conveniently available). Trekking poles help enormously on the uneven climbs and descents, and for river crossings. A GPS, maps, and compass help when the trail is not marked or obvious.

The trail is divided into 300 sections ranging from one- to two-hour rambles near towns to a nine-day stretch in the South Island where all food and equipment must be carried. Thru-hikers take anywhere from

Swingbridge over the Pelorus River, Mount Richmond Forest Park

OPPOSITE
Looking toward Whangarei Heads from Ocean Beach, Northland

three to six months to finish the entire trail, with four to five months being the average. Most people travel southbound, beginning sometime after October. Spring comes later on the South Island, so northbounders need to wait until late November or December to avoid the lambing season (when some sections of the trail are closed) and the snowmelt. Camping is allowed almost everywhere, though permission should be sought from private landowners. The Department of Conservation runs a hut system, with huts liberally sprinkled along the trail. Resupplying is easier on the more populated North Island. On the South Island, you may need to hike longer distances between resupplies, hitch out to a town big enough to have services, or send mail drops.

The trail is being relocated off of roads as easements and permissions become available. But planners do not intend to route it away from towns and roads altogether. By allowing the trail to meander in and out of populated areas, managers have created a recreational resource that introduces visitors and New Zealanders themselves to all aspects of the country's life: not just the natural areas, but the local people and cultures along the way.

It seems a lovely and fitting approach in a land where you can tramp on a track through the whole country and any Kiwi you share a "cuppa" with becomes a newfound friend.

Eastern end of
Herekino Forest, Northland

BIBBULMUN TRACK

Australia

In the Dreamtime, Waugals roamed the land. This was during the sacred time, before living memory, when the earth was young and unformed. Ancestors—human and animal—moved across Australia creating all living things and giving shape to rivers, mountains, and lakes. One of these ancestors was the Waugal, a rainbow serpent, so named because it had the shape of both a rainbow and a serpent. As it moved across southwestern Australia, it created everything we see today, paying especial attention to the waterways in a land that was harsh and dry. Today, the Waugals reside deep beneath some of the springs, which the local Aboriginal people, called the Noongar, consider sacred.

While some Noongar elders are in contact with the Waugals, most people encounter them only at the Darling escarpment, whose edge is said to represent the body of the elusive spirit-creatures. They are also found drawn on the route markers of the Bibbulmun Track, a 621-mile hiking path from Perth to Albany in southwestern Australia.

Visitors to Australia might also encounter a number of other improbable and equally unfamiliar animals. A partial list includes emus, kangaroos, southwestern pygmy possums, quokkas (nocturnal herbivorous marsupials), bandicoots (an insect-eating marsupial), cockatoos and kookaburras (a bird that sounds like a monkey), the occasional python lurking under a shelter floorboard (at least there won't be mice), and the not-uncommon tiger snake (said to be one of the most venomous snakes in the world, but fortunately, not aggressive).

Founded as Australia's answer to the Appalachian Trail, the Bibbulmun has much in common with its role model. Like the AT, the Bibbulmun Track is a walker-only trail. (The Munda Biddi, a parallel long-distance trail to the west, opened for bicyclists in 2013.) While the Bibbulmun does not have nearly as much foot traffic as the AT, both trails share a certain character of community, with a core group of volunteers who maintain the trail. For hikers, the community is centered around a system of 49 huts. As on the AT, towns along or near the trail can be used for resupply, although there are some sections where on-trail towns are farther apart than you'll want to hike without a resupply. Hitchhiking or arranging rides in advance may be necessary.

Like "the long green tunnel" of the Appalachian Trail, the Bibbulmun has long miles of forest, scrub, and brush (there's a reason they call it bush walking). But they do trees differently in Oz. Starting southbound from Kalamunda, the trail's northern terminus, about nine miles east of Perth, the first half of the trail winds through forests of native eucalypti like jarrah, marri, and wandoo, which are only found in this part of Western Australia. Then, the trees switch over to karri (another type of eucalyptus, which can grow to more than 200 feet in height). The trail passes the famous 236-foot-tall Gloucester Tree, the world's second-tallest karri tree, which has a fire-lookout platform built into it. Visitors can climb the 190 feet to the lookout platform via a ladder of steel spikes drilled into the tree's trunk. The climb is straight up and completely exposed: only about 20 percent of those who start actually make it to the top. Farther along the trail, in Walpole-Nornalup National Park, another tree gives visitors a very different opportunity to get close and personal. *Eucalyptus jacksonii*, native to southwest Australia, can grow to a height of 246 feet, live up to 400 years, and is characterized by trunks that are often hollowed out by forest fires. The grand dame is a 400-year-old specimen called the Giant Tingle, a fire-scoured tree whose trunk is surrounded by still-living tissue, despite the fact that the hollow burned into the base is so large that 100 people can fit inside.

Karri Forest,
Bibbulmun Track

FOLLOWING SPREAD
Big Quarrum Beach,
Bibbulmun Track

The trail finishes along the ocean coast near Albany, weaving through a combination of cliffs, coastal heathlands and forests, and beaches. Challenges include struggling over sand dunes, where soft sand makes for slow going, and figuring out how and when to safely cross tidal flats. Rewards include the unfolding seascape views and possible sightings of seals, dolphins, and whales.

Almost all of the Bibbulmun Track is routed through state forests, national parks, and other reserves, with a few small sections of farmland. This is not a mountain experience: the trail's high point is Mount Cooke, which tops out the Darling escarpment at a mere 1,909 feet. That doesn't mean there isn't any climbing: plenty of short steep sections unrelieved by switchbacks would be recognizable to AT hikers as PUDs—"pointless ups and downs." One, nicknamed Cardiac Hill, engenders arguments about whether it's tougher to go up or down. Other challenges have a distinct Aussie accent: the possibility of having to fend off semitame campground kangaroos with a hiking stick, or dodge the occasional charging emu.

The track consists of 58 sections (usually a day's walk apart; sometimes less), and is marked at regular intervals. Campsites containing shelters and tent sites are spaced about seven to 16 miles apart. In the northern half, most campsites have a barbecue pit; open fires are banned in the southern section, and other fire restrictions may apply, especially during the summer. Shelters are free and available on a first-come-first-served basis, so hikers are advised to carry a tent in case shelters are full. Two unusual features: many of the shelters were prefabricated in a prison workshop, then erected by trail volunteers, and some of the privies (also prefabricated in the prison program) are known for their outstanding views.

Hikers should note that motor vehicle access to the trail (no matter what road maps may show) is limited to designated access points only. This is an attempt to limit the spread of *Phytophthora cinnamomi*, a soilborne water mold that causes dieback disease. The spores can be transmitted via vehicle tires, and is of particular concern in this part of Australia, where the native tree species— which support populations of endangered species—are especially vulnerable. Hikers will also see periodic boot-washing stations, where they are asked to rinse off the soles of their boots to prevent carrying spores from one section of trail to another.

The entire walk takes thru-hikers an average of six to eight weeks, but as with most trails, the majority of usage is from hikers out for shorter hikes of two to four days. For thru-hikers, the most popular time to walk the track is during the spring wildflower season (September through November), going from north to south to follow the spring. Fall is the second-best time, going from south to north to stay with the warmer temperatures as long as possible. Winter can be wet, especially in the southern areas. Most locals avoid doing long hikes in the Australian summer, when fire danger is high, temperatures can be brutal, and, even if the Waugals do live under the springs, water will be hard to find.

The name Bibbulmun refers to the Aboriginal Noongar people of southwestern Australia. It is an appropriate name for a long trek: the "walkabout" is an Aboriginal Australian tradition with roots that go back before the dawn of history. As a rite of passage, male Aborigines would undertake wilderness journeys that could last for as long as six months. Later the word was used by white employers to disparagingly explain why Aborigine employees sometimes simply didn't show up for work.

Today, attitudes about walkabouts have changed. Indeed, with the interest in long-distance hiking, one might even say that European culture seems to be coming around to the realization that the Aborigines had the right idea all along. Whatever the hiker's motivation—soul seeking, escape, or simple relaxation—the Bibbulmun Track honors this tradition. The trail gives hikers the opportunity to explore the forests and oceanside ecosystems of this biologically and scenically rich region the way the Aborigines did for thousands of years—on foot. The Waugals will show you the way.

River Road Bridge
over Warren River

OPPOSITE
West Cape Howe,
Bibbulmun Track

MORE LONG WALKS

Almost all long trails are continually in some stage of development: it takes many years to get the necessary easements, put the trail in place, mark it, and write a guidebook about it. By the time that job is done, there are new regulations and land-use issues, some of which necessitate relocation. Most of the trails that follow are in some stage of development—but all have sections that can be hiked today.

Hokkaido Nature Trail, Japan

Japan is a nation of nature lovers—and home to some of the world's longest trails, of which the Hokkaido Nature Trail, at 2,849 miles, is the longest. The mileage is surprising, considering that Hokkaido is only roughly the size of South Carolina. But the trail turns and twists, adding mileage as it takes in glaciers, forests, seascapes, and steaming, volcanic mountains. A hike of the entire trail takes six to seven months—a challenge on an island with short summers and long, cold winters. Most long-distance trekkers break a thru-hike into two seasons.

North Country Trail, United States

At 4,400 miles, the North Country Trail is the longest trail in the US National Scenic Trails System. Still in development, it crosses the northern United States from the New York–Vermont border to the middle of North Dakota. Some of the highlights include New York's Finger Lakes, the waterfalls and gorges of Ohio's Hocking Hills State Park, the walk along Lake Superior, and the grasslands of North Dakota. Small towns form an important part of this trail, and give hikers an opportunity to explore the North Country's history of canals, settlements, and survival in the challenging winters of the north.

Hayduke Trail, United States

This maverick 800-mile-long desert trail is a challenging route through the stunning red rock of the Colorado Plateau in Southern Utah and Northern Arizona. The name honors the late Edward Abbey, and the trail is as rugged and ornery as the famed writer was said to be. Elevations range from 1,800 feet in the Grand Canyon to 11,419 feet on Mount Ellen's south summit—one of the largest elevation differentials of any trail in the world. Much of the trail is not signed or is off-trail, requiring navigation skills, desert hiking know-how, and good physical conditioning. But the rewards are breathtaking: located entirely on public land, the route links Arches, Canyonlands, Capitol Reef, Bryce Canyon, Grand Canyon, and Zion National Parks with Grand Staircase–Escalante National Monument, Glen Canyon National Recreation Area, and numerous national forests, Bureau of Land Management districts, primitive areas, wilderness areas, and wilderness study areas.

Hokkaido Nature Trail, Japan

OPPOSITE
North Country Trail,
Michigan, United States

FOLLOWING SPREAD
Hayduke Trail,
Utah, United States

Sentiero Italia, Italy

OPPOSITE
Via Alpina, Western Europe

FOLLOWING SPREAD
England Coastal Path,
England

Sentiero Italia, Italy

This 3,830-mile route is intended to showcase the entire country by taking a spiraling S-shaped path through the Italian Alps, then turning south to follow the Apennine Mountains to Sicily, followed by a northern jog across the Tyrrhenian Sea to Sardinia and Santa Teresa Gallura, site of the ancient city of Tibula. Highlights include the lovely Dolomites, Tuscan vineyards, and the seascapes of the Amalfi Coast. Like many long-distance trails, this one incorporates sections of preexisting trails, including the Grand Alpine Trail (Grande Traversata delle Alpi), the Ligurian Mountain Trail, and the Tuscan Grand Apennine Trail. The entire route has been hiked, but construction and marking of new connecting sections have not been completed, so hikers wanting to follow a marked and maintained route should choose one of the preexisting sections. It is estimated that it would take about 350 days to complete the entire route.

Via Alpina, Western Europe

One of the longest and newest mountain trails in the world, the Via Alpina is a network of trails intended to showcase the cultures, history, character, and ecology of the entire Alps mountain range. At the core is the

1,500-mile Red Trail, which takes a winding path from Slovenia to Monaco. The other trails in the system—Violet, Yellow, Green, and Blue—are offshoots, each of which departs from and returns to the main trunk line. Added together, the routes total approximately 3,100 miles and 342 stages of alpine hiking. The entire system crosses Slovenia, Austria, Germany, Liechtenstein, Switzerland, Italy, France, and Monaco. The Via Alpina, which is marked and signposted, was finished in 2005.

England Coastal Path, England

The world's newest long-distance trail is slated to open in 2020 and will be the world's longest coastal path at approximately 2,800 miles—give or take. The path was enabled by the passage of the Right of Coastal Access. The new trail will take in already existing seaside routes, including the South West Coast Path, which at 620 miles is currently England's longest hiking trail. Like the South West Coast Path, which follows 19th-century patrol paths formed to protect travelers from the banditry that was rife along the coast, the England Coastal Path will follow a combination of historic routes and newly developed trails. It will also be possible to connect the England Coastal Path with the 870-mile Wales Coast Path, making for almost 3,700 miles of seaside walking.

Great Himalaya Trails, Bhutan, India, Nepal, Pakistan, and Tibet

Even by long-distance standards, the Great Himalaya Trails—a system of hiking routes that traverses the entire Himalayan Range—is an ambitious undertaking, not only for hikers, but for trail promoters. The political and practical realities of the region are daunting. Difficulties include international border crossings, unsettled political situations, permit and guide regulations, and the sheer difficulty of creating a safe and connected route through the highest mountains on earth. At present, the route exists as a loose network of trails, roads, walking paths, and plans. Whether the 2,800-mile system will ever be completed is an open question, but in the meantime, Nepal's 1,056-mile section is the most complete. The route here is split into low and high routes beginning at Kanchenjunga Base Camp and ending on the Tibetan border in Humla. The low route averages about 6,600 feet in elevation, and passes through villages and

towns, making it both a mountain experience and a cultural experience. The high route reaches elevations above 20,000 feet and requires high-mountain trekking experience. Special permits and guides are required to hike outside of the Everest, Annapurna, and Langtang-Helambu regions. To do the entire Nepal section would take about 150 days; most trekkers attempt much smaller sections.

TransPanama Trail, Panama

Hiking in the tropics is not everyone's cup of mango juice. Heat, humidity, sweat, jungles, mud, mosquitoes, and the possibility of meeting creatures ranging from jaguars to the venomous fer-de-lance viper are all part of the fun of attempting to cross Panama from its border with Colombia to its border with Costa Rica. The rewards include encounters with indigenous peoples, canoeing through the rain forest, climbing through the cloud forests of the tropical mountains, coastal walks along the seashore, and following in the footsteps of Spanish conquistadors, who traveled from Peru overland to transport looted gold and silver to the Caribbean and thence to Spain. The mountainous western half of the

Great Himalaya Trails, Nepal

OPPOSITE
TransPanama Trail, Panama

trail opened to hikers in June 2009. Trail maps, markers, and infrastructure are still in the early stages, so unless you're good with a compass and maybe a machete, a guide is recommended. When finished, the trail will be some 700 miles long.

Baekdu-Daegan Trail, South Korea

This hike follows the Baekdu-Daegan ridge, an 870-mile range that forms the geographic backbone of the Korean peninsula. It's also a psycho-spiritual touchstone. The trail begins at Cheonwangbong and ends, for political reasons, 456 miles later at the North Korean border. These mountains are an important national and spiritual symbol, as evidenced by the numerous shrines along the way; a place as imprinted on the Korean collective self-image as the pyramids might be to an Egyptian, or the Champs-Élysées to a Parisian. The mountains are low, topping out at just above 6,200 feet, but steep and challenging. In between huffing and puffing up and down, the trail offers opportunities to stop in at temples and visit, making this a journey that honors Korea's outdoor soul and its living culture.

FOLLOWING SPREAD
Baekdu-Daegan Trail, South Korea

PHOTOGRAPHY CREDITS

© Susan Alcorn: pp. 195 and 198.

© Fiona Barltrop: pp. 56, 57 (right), and 172 (both).

© Tom Bartel: p. 28.

© Mia Battaglia: pp. 84–85, 86, 87, 88–89, and 90 (bottom).

© Karen Berger: pp. 69, 70–71, 72 (all), 73, 90 (top), and 90–91.

© Karen Berger/Catherine Stratton: pp. 13, 22–23, 48, 49, 50–51, 52 (all), 119, 121, 304, 305, 306 (all), and 308–309 (all).

© Dave Bouskill: pp. 224–225 and 273.

© Charles O. Cecil: pp. 64–65, 100 (all), and 106–107 (all).

© John Cleare: pp. 122, 125, and 164.

© Cameron James Cope: pp. 210–211.

© cornfield/Shutterstock.com: p. 61.

© cowardlion/Shutterstock.com: p. 60.

© Evelyne De Boeck: pp. 29, 30–31, 190–191, 192, 317, 318–319, 320, and 321.

© Swapnil Deshpande: p. 165.

© Ditty_about_summer/Shutterstock.com: p. 66.

© Erin Paul Donovan: pp. 284–285.

© Aaron Doss: pp. 186–187, 188–189, 278–279, 291, 292–293, and 296–297 (all).

© Richard Espenant/Shutterstock.com: p. 98.

© Keith Fergus: pp. 58–59 (all).

© Jiri Foltyn/Shutterstock.com: p. 228.

© James Forrest: pp. 205 and 206–207.

© Karen Friedrichs: pp. 236, 238, and 239.

© Ethan Gehl: pp. 110–111, 176–177, 209, and 216–217.

© César González: p. 331.

© Laura Grier: pp. 114–115 and 170–171.

© Blaine Harrington III: pp. 77, 99, 123, 126–127, and 226.

© Kristin Henning: pp. 24, 25, 32 (top right), and 34–35.

© Jan Kozlowski: pp. 16 and 268–269.

© Eric Krukowski: pp. 182–183, 184–185, 212–213 (all), 274–275, 282, 294–295, 299, 300–301, 302–303, and 324 (both).

© Steve Lagreca/Shutterstock.com: p. 54.

© Max Landsberg: pp. 55 and 327 (top).

© Shawn Liebling: pp. 62–63, 94–95, 97, 102–103 (all), and 264–265.

© Valerie Long: pp. 2–3, 159, 160–161, 162–163, 214–215 (both), 232–233, 234, 266–267, and 286 (top left).

© Vincent Mariani: p. 327 (bottom).

© Alexander Mazurkevich/Shutterstock.com: p. 93.

© Leigh McAdam: pp. 208 and 272.

© Melanie Radzicki McManus: pp. 220–221, 242–243, and 252.

© Benjamin Mercer/Shutterstock.com: p. 37.

© John Nguyen/Shutterstock.com: p. 227.

© Phuong D. Nguyen/Shutterstock.com: pp. 26–27.

© David Noyes: pp. 166–167 and 169 (all).

© Ontario Tourism Marketing Partnership Corporation: p. 263.

© photoNN/Shutterstock.com: pp. 40–41.

© pio3/Shutterstock.com: pp. 148–149.

© Daniel Prudek/Shutterstock.com: p. 330.

© Johanna Read: pp. 140, 141, 142–143 (both), 144, and 145 (both).

© RG-vc/Shutterstock.com: p. 57 (left).

© Gary Richardson: pp. 11 and 172–173.

© Stillman Rogers Photography: pp. 36, 39 (both), and 253.

© Cindy Ross: p. 32 (all except top right).

© Sandie Sabaka: pp. 124 (both), 241, 244, and 245.

© Lorenzo Franco Santin: p. 326.

© Stephen Schoof/Garren Creek Photography: pp. 74–75, 78–79, 283, and 286 (bottom left).

© Bart Smith: pp. 1, 80, 81, 82–83, 95, 101, 104, 105 (both), 118, 128–129, 130, 131 (both), 138 (bottom), 139, 222, 223, 246–247, 248–249 (both), 250, 251, 266 (both), 303, and 323.

© Dave Smith: pp. 237, 258, 259, and 260.

© Joseph Sohm/Shutterstock.com: pp. 116–117.

© srinil_photo/Shutterstock.com: p. 322.

© Ryszard Stelmachowicz/Shutterstock.com: p. 38.

© Dan Stone: pp. 5, 76–77, 112–113, 132–133, 135, 136–137, 138 (top), 180–181, 196–197 (both), 199, 201, 202, and 203.

© Reuben Tabner: pp. 174–175 and back cover.

© Te Araroa Trust: pp. 310–311, 312, 313, and 314–315.

© David Tett: pp. 20–21, 43, 44–45, 46, and 47.

© THPStock/Shutterstock.com: pp. 230–231.

© Chris Townsend: pp. 108–109, 146–147, 150–151, and 168–169.

© Esen Tunar: pp. 254–255, 256–257, 280–281, and 328–329 (both).

© Ian Tuttle: p. 292.

© Eric Valentine: pp. 229, 262, and front cover.

© Kelly vanDellen: pp. 7, 286 (top right and bottom right), 288–289, and 336.

© Ryan Weidert: pp. 14–15, 17, 152–153, 154, 155, 156–157, 178–179, 270–271 (both), 276, 324–325, and 335.

© Coen Wubbels/PHOTOCOEN: pp. 8–9, 18–19, 218–219 (all), and 332–333 (all).

First published in the United States of America in 2017
Rizzoli International Publications, Inc.
300 Park Avenue South • New York, NY 10010 • www.rizzoliusa.com

Project Editor: Candice Fehrman • Book Design: Susi Oberhelman • Endpaper Maps: James Daley

The American Hiking Society is the only national organization that promotes and protects foot trails, their surrounding natural areas, and the hiking experience. For more information, please visit www.americanhiking.org.

2017 2018 2019 2020 / 10 9 8 7 6 5 4 3 2 1

Printed in China

ISBN-13: 978-0-8478-6093-7

Library of Congress Catalog Control Number: 2017937206

Page 1: Continental Divide Trail, Colorado, United States • Pages 2–3: Wonderland Trail, Washington, United States
Page 5: Presidential Traverse, New Hampshire, United States • Page 335: Hayduke Trail, Utah, United States
Above: Appalachian Trail, Tennessee, United States

Israel
1. Israel National Trail
2. Jesus Trail

Jordan
3. Petra Trek

Kenya
4. Mount Kenya

Morocco
5. Mount Toubkal

South Africa
6. Otter Trail

Tanzania
7. Mount Kilimanjaro

*This map is for illustrative purposes only.
Trails are not shown to scale and are not intended for navigational purposes.

China
1. Great Wall of China

Japan
2. Shikoku Pilgrimage
3. Kumano Kodō
4. Mount Fuji
5. Hokkaido Nature Trail

Nepal
6. Helambu-Langtang Trek
7. Annapurna Circuit
8. Everest Base Camp Trek
9. Great Himalaya Trails

South Korea
10. Baekdu-Daegan Trail

Tibet
11. Mount Kailash

*This map is for illustrative purposes only. Trails are not shown to scale and are not intended for navigational purposes.